T0009444

No Limits

No Limits

EMBRACING THE *Miraculous*

DONNA SPARKS

BRIDGE
LOGOS

Newberry, FL 32669

Bridge-Logos
Newberry, FL 32669

No Limits:
Embracing the Miraculous
by Donna Sparks

Copyright© 2019 by Donna Sparks

All rights reserved. Under International Copyright Law, no part of this publication may be reproduced, stored, or transmitted by any means—electronic, mechanical, photographic (photocopy), recording, or otherwise—without written permission from the publisher.

Printed in the United States of America.

Library of Congress Catalog Card Number: 2019900884

International Standard Book Number: 978-1-61036-402-7

Cover/Interior design by Kent Jensen | knail.com

All Scripture quotations, unless otherwise indicated, are taken from the Holy Bible, New International Version®, NIV®. Copyright ©1973, 1978, 1984, 2011 by Biblica, Inc.® Used by permission of Zondervan. All rights reserved worldwide. www.zondervan.com The "NIV" and "New International Version" are trademarks registered in the United States Patent and Trademark Office by Biblica, Inc.®

Scripture quotations marked (NASB) are taken from the New American Standard Bible®, Copyright © 1960,1962,1963,1968,1971,1972,1973,1975, 1977,1995 by The Lockman Foundation. Used by permission. All rights reserved.

Scripture quotations marked (NLT) are taken from the New Living Translation, copyright © 1996, 2004, 2015 by Tyndale House Foundation. Used by permission of Tyndale House Publishers, Inc., Carol Stream, Illinois 60188. All rights reserved.

Scripture quotations marked (KJV) are from the King James Version of the Bible.

Literary Agent and Editor,
L. Edward Hazelbaker
11907 S. Sangre Road
Perkins, OK 74059
E-mail: l.edward@thewornkeyboard.com

Endorsements

No Limits speaks to those crying out for divine interruption. Donna Sparks perfectly illustrates how people with hungry hearts can position themselves to receive the miraculous.

—LARRY DUGGER, Pastor and author of
40 Days to Defeat Your Past

Sometimes in the middle of the muddle we call life, we need a reminder that miracles are still possible. In *No Limits: Embracing the Miraculous,* author Donna Sparks uses her words and heart-touching stories to pull back the curtain of the mundane to reveal sparkling gifts from the hand of our generous, miracle-working God. If you need fresh hope for your *impossible* situation, *No Limits* is your next read.

—DR. JODI DETRICK, author of *The Jesus-Hearted Woman: 10 Leadership Qualities for Enduring & Endearing Influence*

Donna Sparks embraces the supernatural because she has experienced the supernatural! Many would have shackled Donna with limitations because of her past. But Donna encountered the miraculous—God set her free and gave her abundant life. Now, whether she is ministering in a small county jail or standing in some of the most prestigious churches in America, she lives in the miraculous. *No Limits: Embracing the Miraculous* is God's story being lived out in Donna's life and ministry.

—RANDY CARTER, Pastor, Northside Assembly, Jackson, TN

Dedication

THIS BOOK IS dedicated to my two precious miracles from God—my daughters.

Haley and Hannah, you make this mama's heart overflow with joy. I am so proud of you, and I am thrilled to see how you are both allowing God to use you for His glory!

Thank you for your words of love and encouragement. You both are wise beyond your years.

Foreword

I AM A self-proclaimed book-a-holic. I have at any one time various books not yet read. So when Donna Sparks asked me to endorse her book, I thought, "Oh no, not another book." But as soon as I started to read *No Limits: Embracing the Miraculous*, I was hooked. And you will be, too.

Donna writes with clarity, and I love her illustrations. The term "miracles" is often used and hyped by people in an exaggerated way, but Donna shares that true miracles are real and within the reach of anyone. She has lived out a *no limits* lifestyle herself, and she is helping others to do the same.

I work with those who have overcome serious life-controlling problems, who feel they have no future because of their past. I'm going to order copies of this book and put it in their hands. If you identify with this, or know others who do, join me in recommending this book or purchasing copies to give away.

When following Christ, the only limits that exist are the ones we put on ourselves. In this book Donna Sparks makes a strong biblical case that there are possibilities for anyone to live in the miraculous and be used of God, and those possibilities are limitless!

—Don Wilkerson, Author, Pastor, and
Co-Founder of Teen Challenge International
and Times Square Church, NYC

Table of Contents

Introduction

MY HUSBAND AND I once started to watch a fictional TV show called *Limitless*. It was about a man who discovered a pill that would unlock parts of a person's brain that are normally unused. After taking the pill he began to notice that his previous mental and physical limitations were totally gone. He could do things that others could only dream of doing.

The man was amazed by his newfound abilities. He could read all kinds of books and other materials and instantly use what he read to do incredible things. He simply had no limits when it came to the use of his mind. His newfound abilities gave him tremendous control over his destiny and the world around him.

It all seemed to be going well for the man as he took advantage of his opportunities. But then he discovered that the pill was causing irreversible damage to his body. And in fact, it was rapidly killing him. But soon after that discovery, he was approached by a man who had developed a shot that, when used monthly, would reverse the deterioration of his health and allow him to continue to use his *super pill.*

The man who developed the shot was willing to administer the shot to him on a monthly basis provided that the newly *unlimited man* would do his evil bidding. Things of course went from bad to worse as the fictional character had to compromise his own morals to obtain the life-preserving shot. Soon he began to wish he had never even heard of such a pill.

How many times in our own lives have we wished for an easy way to supercharge our own abilities? And wouldn't it be amazing to find a pill that would enable us to overcome all our weaknesses and limitations? It would be great to have no physical or emotional weaknesses to deal with. It would be fabulous to have no fleshly or mental limitations keeping us from being able to fulfill all our dreams.

Unfortunately, though, our lives are not fictional, and the solutions we attempt to apply to ourselves often end up introducing even more complications into our lives.

This is real life that we're living. And real life has real challenges. There is no magic pill for us to take to rid ourselves of the limitations and challenges we experience. But I have good news to share, and I share it as often and with as many as I can.

Here's the good news:

We have a heavenly Father who cares and looks over us every day—24/7.

We have a Savior who left heaven some 2,000 years ago to live among us and finish His work of redeeming us in our weaknesses and sins.

And the Holy Spirit, who now lives with us, is going throughout the entire earth right now to not only convince people of their needs but also lead them in rising above every limitation that can be placed upon them.

We may be limited in our abilities. We may be limited by our circumstances or our weaknesses. But God is not limited by any of them. And because of that, we don't need a magic pill or any other thing that mankind can concoct to enable us to rise above the limitations with which we are all so familiar.

We simply need to come to grips with our limitations, understand them, deal with them, commit them to God, and obediently yield to God's work in us.

God desires to do amazing things in our lives. He wants to do them *for* us—for our benefit—and *through* us—for the benefit of others. The Lord provided many promises for us in the Bible, and we know Him as the one who is *"able to do immeasurably more than all we ask or imagine, according to his power that is at work within us"* (Ephesians 3:20).

Our Savior's mind is unlimited. His knowledge, wisdom, and understanding are unlimited. His power is unlimited. There will never be any lack in Him, and He wants us to trust in that. He wants us to put our faith in Him and believe Him for miracles in our lives and the lives of others.

God can do all things, and we need to move beyond our limitations to let Him do His work.

God lives and breathes in the miraculous. His handiwork is all around us. He made us. He made *"the heavens and the earth, the sea, and all that is in them"* (Exodus 20:11). Since He has that kind of ability there is nothing that limits Him from doing anything He wants to do today. And there is also no limit to what He can do through us—through those who follow, believe, and trust in Him.

We must never limit what God can do in us and through us. The following statement was among the last words spoken by Jesus to His disciples prior to His crucifixion:

> *Very truly I tell you, whoever believes in me will do the works I have been doing, and they will do even greater things than these, because I am going to the Father.* (John 14:12)

God lives in the miraculous, and He wants us to live in it too. He wants us to live above our own earthly and fleshly limitations.

We may be faced with many limitations here on earth. We may live with many weaknesses. But as we follow close to God, and as we place our faith in Him, we can trust Him to enable us to rise above the limitations and weaknesses that plague us in the natural. We can trust Him to raise us up beyond them all to live and function in the realm of the miraculous.

In the miraculous, we who are so limited and weak will see God do what He does so well. He will work in us and through us to lead others to God for solutions to their own limitations and weaknesses. We will see bodies healed. We will see spirits delivered. We will see all manner of solutions brought to the most complex and pitiful issues of humanity.

And we will see the greatest miracle of all—lives saved as they are brought to Jesus.

INTRODUCTION

As you read this book, ask the Holy Spirit to open your eyes, give you wisdom, and increase your faith as He begins to encourage you to rise above the earthly limitations you experience to walk in His unlimited power.

—Donna

CHAPTER 1

From Anointing to Appointing

THE UNLIMITED POWER of God to perform miracles in our lives and the lives of others is the primary theme in this book. So it may seem strange to start the book by talking about being chosen and appointed to our work as Christian believers. But when it comes to God's intention for His followers to not only embrace the miraculous but also share God's miraculous nature with the world around them, it all starts here.

It is no small miracle that God would choose you and me to carry His message. And I've come to believe that if He could not only call me to His work but then also actually have the patience and muscle to equip me for it, I can never doubt God's power.

Having lived my own life—having come to know myself pretty well over time—I've decided that setting the world in motion was not nearly as miraculous as what God has done in me.

If you know Jesus as your personal Savior—if you have been spiritually reborn—and if you have any understanding about how God has worked in your life up to this point, you have already experienced the miraculous.

However, even if you have not yet responded to the call of the Holy Spirit to repent and turn your life over to Jesus, but you have seen God's love revealed in the lives of others, you also have seen God's miraculous power at work.

You've experienced and seen the miracle of salvation. You have already come in contact with the miraculous. Now embrace it and see what God can do in your life.

I think one of the most difficult lessons I have had to learn in ministry is that an anointing does not necessarily mean—or is not always equal to—an appointing. In other words, just because God has anointed me to do something does not mean I have automatically been appointed to start doing it right away. I will explain what I mean by that.

I'm using the word, *anointed*, in the sense of being chosen. I'm using the word, *appointed*, in the sense of being elevated to a position of work or responsibility.

Although in Scripture we can read about some people being both anointed (or chosen for a task) and appointed to a position (elevated and released to do the work) at the same time—witness the anointing and appointing of Jehu as king of Israel[1]—time often passes between the two actions.

---

1   2 Kings 9:1-13.

And living through the period between the two can be challenging for someone like me, who wants to move quickly into the work I feel called to do.

When Jehu was anointed king over the northern ten tribes of Israel (Samaria), the men who were with him immediately accepted him as king (acknowledged his anointing—God's choice), and they joined Jehu as he went about establishing himself in his position.

In the case of many others who have been chosen by God for certain tasks, though, there have sometimes been long periods of time between them being anointed and them actually fulfilling the callings that were placed upon them and stepping into their positions.

I believe many times when God calls people to a work—and this is most certainly true of me—they often feel like they are supposed to *hit the ground running*, so to speak. Since God has anointed us in our calling, we feel like we should quickly go about undertaking the work He has called us to do.

We may envision ourselves standing on a stage as the heavenly music begins to play. The stage curtains open, and we—with all our talents and giftedness—are immediately revealed to the world. However, moving quickly from being anointed for a task to actually fulfilling our calling may not be in God's plan for us—and for good cause.

My daughter recently graduated from high school. She has decided that her calling is to become a registered nurse. I'm thrilled for her, but I'll tell you right now that there is no way she is coming near me with a needle! She hasn't been trained as a nurse yet.

If she were to try to draw blood or give someone an injection right now, I'm afraid it would go very badly for everyone involved. She must be trained and prepared for what is ahead. If she tried to jump into her calling without being prepared for her work, she would fail.

I think back to a story in chapter sixteen of First Samuel. God sent Samuel out to anoint the next king after He had rejected Saul. There was a man in Bethlehem named Jesse, who had several sons, and God told Samuel to go to Bethlehem because He had chosen one of Jesse's sons to be the next king.

When Jesse and his sons presented themselves before Samuel, Samuel first noticed Jesse's son, Eliab. He was tall and evidently looked the part to Samuel. But even though Samuel thought Eliab would make a fine king, God rejected him.

> But the Lord said to Samuel, "Do not consider his appearance or his height, for I have rejected him. The Lord does not look at the things people look at. People look at the outward appearance, but the Lord looks at the heart." (1 Samuel 16:7)

One by one, Jesse had each of his sons pass before Samuel, and God rejected each of them. Perplexed, Samuel then asked Jesse if he had any more sons.

> "There is still the youngest," Jesse answered. "He is tending the sheep." (v.11b)

Samuel then told Jesse to send for his youngest son, David.

And when David arrived, the Lord told Samuel that David was the one He had chosen.

So Samuel took the horn of oil and anointed him in the presence of his brothers, and from that day on the Spirit of the Lord came powerfully upon David. (v.13a)

Can you imagine how David must have felt?

It was just a normal day as he was in the field tending the sheep. Then he was called from the field and anointed to be king. I wonder if David thought he would immediately be taken to the palace and crowned king.

The Bible doesn't say, but I'm sure David wondered how things were all going to work out since Saul was still the reigning king.

Well, in time David was indeed moved into the palace, but it was not to be king; it was to serve King Saul as a musician.[2] The position of palace musician—hired to play the lyre to sooth Saul's mind whenever he felt emotionally tormented—probably wasn't the life David envisioned after being anointed by Samuel.

But that is how God introduced David to life in the palace.

There is not complete agreement on the time line, but many Bible scholars believe David was fifteen years old when God had Samuel anoint David in front of David's family. If that is true, then it was a full twenty-two years later before David was accepted as king by the entire united kingdom of both Judah and Israel.

David was first anointed by Samuel (signifying God's choice) when David was a teenager. But it was many years later, only after Saul died—and after David had married two wives and had

---

2   1 Samuel 16:14-23.

a group of men who followed him—when he actually took his position as a king.

Then David was anointed king a second time, but that time he was anointed by the men of Hebron to be king over only the tribe of Judah.[3] More time passed before David was anointed yet a third time and recognized as king by the rest of the tribes of Israel.[4]

Many years passed for David between being chosen by God to be king and actually rising to the position.

According to what we read in verse four of Second Samuel chapter five, David was thirty years old when he was appointed to be king over the tribe of Judah. And he reigned over only Judah for seven-and-a-half years before the other tribes of Israel appointed him to be king over them.[5]

David was anointed—chosen by God to be king—at a young age, but his actual appointing to that work came much later. Much happened in David's life following the anointing administered by Samuel, and it is no overstatement for us to say that God clearly used the intervening years to prepare David for what He had anointed him to do.

I recently shared this chapter's message with a women's group. For an object lesson, I searched all over to find a roll of 35 mm film. Who knew they were so hard to come by these days?

---

3   2 Samuel 2:1-4.
4   2 Samuel 5:1-3.
5   "David was thirty years old when he became king, and he reigned forty years. In Hebron he reigned over Judah seven years and six months, and in Jerusalem he reigned over all Israel and Judah thirty-three years" (2 Samuel 5:4). See also 1 Kings 2:10-11.

In our meeting, I held up the roll of film and asked if any of the young ladies there knew what I had in my hand. Of course none of them did. When I explained what it was, they surely must have thought I was a dinosaur in this modern age of technology.

Today we can snap a picture with our cell phone, and someone in another country can see the picture less than a minute later. Further, none of those young ladies had ever been limited to taking only between twelve and thirty-six pictures before having to change out a roll of film in her camera!

Today we take any number of digital pictures at one time—many more than we need. We can then instantly view them. And if we don't like them, we can delete them quickly and start over. But back in the *good old days* we were limited when it came to how many pictures we could take, and seeing the results was anything but instant.

We were much more selective with the photos we snapped back then, because after we had taken those photos, we were just getting started.

Next we had to take them to a store where the exposed roll of film could be sent off to be developed. It was usually about a week before we would get back an envelope containing developed pictures, and we would quickly open it just hoping some of the pictures turned out well.

As I reflected on this, I thought to myself, "It's no wonder we live in a world that is so impatient when we are all programmed to expect immediate gratification and excess."

And considering that, it's no wonder that we get so frustrated when God anoints us to do something for Him and then have to wait to rise to our appointment. But God knows exactly what He is doing.

For just a moment, let's pretend *we* are rolls of 35 mm film. God begins to impress images on the film of our hearts. They are images of our future, and they display our potential. Inside we know what He is calling us to be, but on the outside—to everyone around us—we just look like rolls of film.

We are so excited when God chooses us and begins to reveal to us what He wants us to do, but then something mystifying happens. Like a roll of film, God takes us into the obscurity of the darkroom.

Just when we think our anointing is going to be revealed—we're about to go to work and be used in amazing ways—we find ourselves in the dark where no one can even see us.

Like pictures being processed and printed, we may go through a period of time when we feel incomplete and sometimes even invisible as we wait for God to elevate us to our calling. But throughout the entire process—while we wait for God to reveal His intentions for us to the world—God is *developing* us.

A roll of film can't understand the process of developing, and it has no idea of the potential spooled up within it. But the photographer certainly has high expectations of the film's value, and the entire process through which the film is subjected in order to bring out its full value is well known to the expert developer.

Sometimes we don't understand the steps in God's developing process in our lives, but God certainly does.

When God anoints us for His purpose, we can be assured that He will *prepare* us for what He has called us to do. And even though we may have an idea of what we can become as we follow our callings, there is no way for us to fully comprehend what God can and will do through us once we are fully developed by His miracle-working hands.

Clearly, allowing God to develop us requires patience on our part. Patience is not necessarily one of my natural virtues, but I'm learning more and more about its value in my life.

And when it comes to the value of patience, think of this: While a roll of film is being developed, if the door to the darkroom is opened too soon, the images on the film will be completely ruined. If the film and photo paper are exposed to light (revealed or seen openly in light) too soon, they will be ruined forever.

Before being fully developed, a roll of film's exposure to the light of day will render it useless. But once completely developed, all the pictures within it—all the potential that was waiting to be revealed—can finally be seen and become a blessing to many.

Our attempts to step into a position before we have been fully prepared for our work can render us ineffective and sometimes, yes, useless. We must be patient and submit to the whole development process that God is using to prepare us for our callings.

Now let's go beyond constructing a simple awareness of our *need* for development, and let's consider what God is actually developing *within* us.

Certainly we must expect God to develop the things in our lives that will work in tandem with the anointing He has placed upon us. And one of the most important things God is developing within us is *character*. Without good character we will not succeed in doing what God has planned for us to do.

Several years ago, I heard Dr. George O. Wood[6] speak, and I heard him make this statement:

> The gift that is on you will destroy you if the character within you can't sustain you.

I wrote that statement down in my notebook, and I've never forgotten it.

Being a person of trusted character can involve many things, but there are two important ingredients that definitely cannot be overlooked. One is humility. The other is wisdom.

When it comes to humility, that's not always easy for us to learn or accept. God must sometimes crush a lot of pride and selfish desires within us in order for us to become all He wants us to be.

Such crushing is never pleasant, but the results prove its worth. And it's truly a miracle when God takes prideful, self-centered people and turns them into humble, self-sacrificing servants of Christ.

We've all heard of that annoying guy who just graduated college and decided to teach everyone how to do the jobs they had already been doing for thirty years. We usually call that guy a *know-it-all*. People like that are seen as lacking the practical maturity that comes from years of experience.

---

6 Dr. George O. Wood, former General Superintendent of the General Council of the Assemblies of God, USA, who served as General Superintendent from 2007 to 2017.

Presenting oneself to others as a know-it-all certainly isn't an example of humility, and it negatively affects a person's character.

We must seek to have the kind of humble character that God desires us to have. And we must acknowledge that being put into positions too soon could cause us to become arrogant or puffed up. God knows that, so we must be patient and let God make us vessels of character and honor—and in His own timing.

When it comes to wisdom, it is something that is often obtained only through long periods of personal, spiritual growth. Wisdom is not something we're born with. Wisdom is gained through not only having a desire for understanding and knowledge but also by learning over time—sometimes by personal and painful experiences—how understanding and knowledge are to be correctly applied.

I'm reminded of one of Joseph's experiences recorded in the thirty-seventh chapter of Genesis. Joseph was another person who had to go through a long period of developing before God could use him in the way He had planned. Remember what happened when God revealed Joseph's calling to him in a dream? He told the dream to his brothers.

> *He said to them, "Listen to this dream I had: We were binding sheaves of grain out in the field when suddenly my sheaf rose and stood upright, while your sheaves gathered around mine and bowed down to it."* (Genesis 37:6-7)

The Bible tells us that Joseph's brothers hated Joseph because they knew he was their father's favorite. They couldn't even speak a kind word to him (v.4). So their response to Joseph's dream was no surprise.

His brothers said to him, "Do you intend to reign over us? Will
you actually rule us?" And they hated him all the more because
of his dream and what he had said. (v.8)

The Bible doesn't say anything about Joseph actually being anointed, but it is clear that God chose Joseph at an early age to take upon himself some very important tasks. God was beginning to reveal to Joseph his future. But one can argue that Joseph didn't use much wisdom when dealing with his calling.

I have thought to myself many times, "What a goofy move, Joseph. You were just asking for it."

But if we're not careful, we may find ourselves doing some things that many would consider just as goofy.

We can become so excited and thrilled with the things that God is doing in our lives that we want to tell the world. But depending on who we are telling, and how we are telling it, we can look like we are just being arrogant when we talk about what God is revealing to us.

Sometimes when God lets us know He is calling us for a special task, we just need to quietly keep it to ourselves until the right time for God to reveal it to the world. Even Mary, the mother of Jesus—who had the most exciting, miraculous news to tell when God chose her to give birth to the promised Messiah—did not broadcast the news to everyone she met.

She showed wisdom.

Progressing from our anointing to our appointing may be a quick process, or it can take a while. We may be under development for our work for days, weeks, months, or even years. Regardless, though, as I understand it God's purpose in this is two-fold:

First, God wants us to have the understanding and knowledge it will require for us to do the work He has called us to do. And second, He knows we must be able to do His work with humility and wisdom.

We need to know when to act, how to act, when to speak, what to say, and how to do all of them with a humble heart before God and the people around us. God knows our needs, and He understands both our strengths *and* our weaknesses. He understands that we need to know what we're doing.

God knows we need to draw from experience. He knows when we need to work on our humility. And He knows our need of wisdom.

The Lord is always working to develop our abilities and attitudes. And He often does it in miraculous ways. When we finally learn what we needed to learn, and when we become what God wants us to be—when He sees we are ready to be elevated to our assigned tasks—we will be ready for our appointment.

On that day we will begin doing all those things He anointed us to do.

CHAPTER 2

Faith and Persistence

LET ME JUST say I have one of the most loving and caring husbands on the planet. He spoils me rotten. As I began to write this book he blessed me by sending me to a little fishing cabin out on a lake in Rising Fawn, Georgia for inspiration and time alone. For seven days it was just me, Jesus, and nature.

I was in awe of the perfection and beauty of the place. The cozy little cabin sits at the foothills of a majestic mountain. It was nicely appointed. Its decor was both rustic and luxurious. And a deck attached to the cabin extended out over the water. It surely provided the perfect place to cast a line in hopes of catching a prize-winning fish.

Before I traveled to that small piece of heaven in Georgia, I decided to look it up online to read the reviews.

There were raving reviews about the fishing at the cabin. People boasted of catching Bass, Crappie, Catfish, and Sunfish right from the cabin's deck. Even though I planned to spend most of my time writing, I decided to throw my fishing pole and tackle box into my Jeep before leaving home.

When I arrived at the cabin I looked down from the deck and saw fish of every size swimming below. So I decided to get up the next morning and try my luck. I awoke to an incredible view of the lake. Low clouds were drifting across the mountaintop, and as I viewed the beauty of nature I was in awe of God's splendor in His creation.

As soon as I had my morning coffee and prayer time, I got my fishing tackle and anxiously baited a hook. I expectantly cast my line out across the lake and waited patiently.

Nothing happened—not a nibble, not a bite, nothing. I reeled in my line and cast again. Still nothing. I found myself casting repeatedly to no avail. I changed depth. I changed bait. I changed spots over and over again. I was having no luck at all. So I gave up and went back inside the cabin to write.

But a couple hours later I was drawn outside again by the beauty of the lake and the desire to catch a fish.

I cast again, waited, and still nothing. I continued the process so many times I lost count. Even though I had no luck catching a fish, something compelled me to continue to cast my fishing line into the water and wait. But it seemed that I was not going to catch a single fish.

"Why am I even trying?" I asked myself.

I read the reviews about the cabin. I read stories of the fish so many others had caught there. And then when I myself came to the water's edge I witnessed with my own two eyes multitudes of fish swimming in the lake.

But I couldn't catch a fish.

I was discouraged, but I know from experience that sometimes the fish just aren't biting. And clearly, that was one of those times. However, I also knew I had all the right equipment, so I persisted. I continued to cast and reel hoping for the slightest tug at the end of the fishing line.

Sometimes I wonder why it is so hard for us to persist in faith when it comes to spiritual things. We can be so determined in our dogged pursuit of earthly things, but when it comes to persisting in faith until we see God move in our lives and situations, many of us throw in the towel after sending up the first prayer. I have to admit that I've been guilty of that.

I stood on the deck and continued to cast my fishing line out into the water. I refused to give up. And then my mind shifted to thinking about how easily I sometimes give up when it comes to believing God for bringing about change and doing miraculous things in my life, or in the lives of others.

Oh, but how persistently I continued to cast my fishing line into the lake for something worth so much less!

As I began to think about the things that caused me to persevere in my effort to catch fish from the lake, I came to realize that there are some parallels between that and how I pursue the things of God. And I reminded myself that if I have faith in my abilities to catch fish, I should certainly have faith in God to perform miracles and do anything else He certainly has the ability and desire to do.

I READ ABOUT IT

I read about other people who caught fish in that lake, and it inspired me. I *believed* their accounts of catching all kinds of fish, and I determined to catch some too.

We should likewise be inspired when we go to the Word of God and read many accounts of how Jesus and His followers made the lame to walk, caused the blind to see, healed lepers, and performed countless other miracles.

And as Christ's followers today, we should be determined to not only receive the miracle-working power of God into our own lives but also see it bring change to the lives of others.

Let the Scriptures inspire *you*:

Very truly I tell you, whoever believes in me will do the works I have been doing, and they will do even greater things than these, because I am going to the Father. And I will do whatever you ask in my name, so that the Father may be glorified in the Son. You may ask me for anything in my name, and I will do it. (John 14:12-14)

The Word of God is far more reliable than any written account of some unknown fisherman's tales. The Word of God is the absolute Truth! We can trust what the Bible says.

If we want to experience miracles in our own lives, we can be inspired by reading about what Jesus did, what His disciples did, and what multitudes of Jesus' followers have done throughout church history. Jesus and His faithful followers set an example for us. They have shown us that miracles happen when we believe.

By reading the Bible we come to understand that Jesus wants us to be involved in—and to live in—the miraculous, especially when it comes to ministry to others. That should build a hunger within us to increase our faith and persevere in doing more for God.

I SAW IT

I *saw* fish in the lake. I knew without a doubt there were fish in the lake because I stood on the deck a day earlier and saw them swimming around.

How often have we seen people in need of a miracle? And how many times have we ourselves seen people receive miracles? I can think of more than a few times when I've seen God move in a powerful way and people were healed. I witnessed it with my own eyes.

I've experienced divine healing in my own body and received deliverance from the enemies of my soul. And I've seen God move in miraculous ways to not only save and deliver people from destruction but to also direct their paths over time. So I know beyond a doubt that God is willing and able to heal, change a situation, or perform a miracle, because I've seen Him do it many times.

Here is the way the apostle John began his first letter:

> *That which was from the beginning, which we have heard, which we have seen with our eyes, which we have looked at and our hands have touched—this we proclaim concerning the Word of life.*

> *The life appeared; we have seen it and testify to it, and we proclaim to you the eternal life, which was with the Father and has appeared to us.*

We proclaim to you what we have seen and heard, so that you also may have fellowship with us. And our fellowship is with the Father and with his Son, Jesus Christ. We write this to make our joy complete. (1 John 1:1-4)

John was direct with his readers. He told them in no uncertain terms that he and the others who walked with Jesus knew what they were talking about. The readers could have confidence in what they said.

They could believe their stories. They could believe their teachings. And they could believe the miracles they recorded. Why? They could believe them because they had seen the Lord and His work—they had first-hand experience.

They testified to what they saw, and that was in part what drove them. It drove them to want to please God, but it also drove them to bring God's power to bear in the lives of others. We also should be emboldened by what we have already seen God do, and it should inspire us to want to see and do more.

I KNOW FISH DON'T ALWAYS BITE

I continued to cast out the fishing line even though I knew the fish weren't biting. I wouldn't give up.

I understood that a fisher's timing isn't always going to fall into alignment with the appetite of the fish. But not even that knowledge would stop me from trying to catch a fish. Why? Because I'm a fisher. People who are not fishers may not fully understand this, but fishers fish. That's what they do.

Of course fishers aren't dumb. They get to know their prey. They know in a general way where the fish are more likely to be and when they are more likely to be hungry enough to take the bait. But despite all their knowledge and efforts, they are sometimes disappointed because the fish don't cooperate.

Sometimes the timing is just off for those of us who fish, and we're not exactly sure why.

We know it is in God's nature to save, heal, and deliver. And we know He wants to work through His followers to perform miracles, signs, and wonders. If Jesus worked through His disciples, He will work through us, but in every instance we must seek after and yield to *His timing*.

Fishers know they must be patient to be successful. And when it comes to our success at being used by God to reveal the Lord's miraculous plans and deeds to those who need to receive them, we too must be patient.

If we refuse to give in to disappointment when things don't go the way we planned or expected—if we continue to exercise our faith and patiently serve God—we will be there when the time is right for God to manifest His glory.

I HAVE THE RIGHT EQUIPMENT

As I stood there on the deck with fishing pole in hand, I knew I had the *right* equipment to catch a fish that day. But it was not to be.

I finally decided that if I were to catch a fish out of that lake it would have to be at another time. I know how to catch fish, but the timing was off that day. The fish weren't letting me catch them. They weren't impressed with my qualifications, and quite frankly, they couldn't care less what kind of equipment I was using.

The fish were having none of it.

Sometimes it's like that in ministry. Sometimes a Christian has all the qualifications and is fully equipped to bring a miracle to the lives of those in need, but they, too, are having none of it. And for those of us who daily yearn to bring salvation, healing, and deliverance to others, that is one of the most frustrating things we can experience.

Sometimes, regardless of our efforts, we are left to being satisfied with simply knowing that we gave our best effort and applied all the faith, knowledge, and wisdom we possess—used all the equipment provided to us by the Holy Spirit.

While patiently waiting for the time to be right, we must trust not only the equipment we have but also—and even more so—the supplier of that spiritual tackle. Never doubt the Lord's abilities and goals.

Trust in what God has done in the past, and believe that He can and will do the same or similar things both now and in the future, because God never changes.

Jesus Christ is the same yesterday and today and forever.
                                                        (Hebrews 13:8)

Every good and perfect gift is from above, coming down from the Father of the heavenly lights, who does not change like shifting shadows.   (James 1:17)

I the Lord do not change . . .   (Malachi 3:6)

We know we have the right equipment. We have the Bible. We have the truth. And we have the Holy Spirit to empower and guide us. The Bible tells us that the same power that raised Christ from the dead lives in us.

Here is what Paul wrote to the Ephesians:

I pray that the eyes of your heart may be enlightened in order that you may know the hope to which he has called you, the riches of his glorious inheritance in his holy people, and his incomparably great power for us who believe.

That power is the same as the mighty strength he exerted when he raised Christ from the dead and seated him at his right hand in the heavenly realms, far above all rule and authority, power and dominion, and every name that is invoked, not only in the present age but also in the one to come. (Ephesians 1:18-21)

If we have surrendered our lives to God and are diligently following Him, we are equipped to see His power move in and through us if we don't stop *fishing*.

Demonstrate faith and persistence!

I'm reminded of another fishing story. It's in the Bible, and it's about someone else who wasn't having any luck catching fish.

It was early in Jesus' ministry, and a large number of people had followed Jesus to the shore of the Lake of Gennesaret, where He was teaching them. In Luke chapter five we read about Jesus getting into Simon Peter's boat as Peter and other fishermen were washing their nets after fishing all night. Jesus asked Peter to put out a little from the shore so He could teach the people from the boat.

Then after Jesus finished teaching, He told Peter, *"Put out into deep water, and let down the nets for a catch"* (v. 4).

Peter answered Jesus by telling Him that he and the others had fished all night and hadn't caught anything. *"But because you say so,"* he said to Jesus, *"I will let down the nets"* (v. 5).

Peter was a fisherman by trade. He had all kinds of experience when it came to catching fish. So he may have had some doubts about trusting Jesus when it came to deciding when to fish. Jesus, after all, was not a professional fisherman. But we can assume that Peter was extremely impressed with and influenced by Jesus' teachings and deeds.

Peter had already experienced Jesus' power to heal, when one day Jesus healed Peter's mother-in-law of a high fever at Peter's house.[7] And that evening, while Jesus was still at Peter's house, many people were brought to Jesus, and Jesus healed them there. And at the same time, Peter also witnessed Jesus driving out demons from people who had been demon possessed.[8]

So it's not really hard to imagine that Peter would do as Jesus instructed.

Peter did as the Lord asked. He launched out into the deep waters, and Peter soon found out that he had with him all he needed to enable him to see, experience, and enjoy a miracle.

Jesus was in the boat!

Peter lowered the nets into the water, and to his surprise, when he and his crew began pulling the nets back in, the nets were filled so full that they began to break. So they signaled to their partners in the other boat—James and John—to come and help them. Soon both boats were so full of fish that they began to sink! (vv. 7-10)

---

7   Luke 4:38-39.
8   Luke 4:40-41.

What if Peter had refused to go back out into the deep water and cast his nets one more time? I think many times we might be right on the verge of seeing our miracle, but we just give up.

We have to be persistent!

When we're discouraged we must remind ourselves of Jesus' promises and His character. We also must respond to Him with obedience. And something that will inspire us to do that is for us to build up our faith by reading and studying His Holy Word.

Through faithfully following Christ and becoming confident in what we learn from the Bible as we are taught by the Holy Spirit, we will not only find faith but also learn to exhibit it. We will see God's will accomplished in our lives and ministries.

And we will exhibit persistence in all we do because we know that Jesus is in our boat, too.

I fished several times during the week of my retreat at the cabin. I tried fishing in the morning, late in the evening, at noon, at dusk, and at dawn. I used various types of tackle to fish for all the types of fish I knew were in the lake. I ended up only catching one Sunfish.

But I sure was proud of that fish.

My persistence and refusal to give up led to me finally pulling a nice-sized fish out of that lake. I might not have caught a boat-full, but I did catch something. If I had given up after the first cast, I would have caught nothing. And if I had given up after my entire first fishing session I would have caught nothing.

I believed it was just a matter of time before I would catch a fish. I had faith in it, and I persisted in that belief.

Of course considering everything, whether or not I caught a fish is a minor thing compared to the world's need to experience the miracle-working hand of God.

When it comes to demonstrating our faith and persistently following and working for Christ, it seems to me that if we could only look at it the same way we look at fishing—or the way we look at anything else to which we are truly committed—we would not only experience more personal miracles but also be more effective in bringing the miracle-working power of God to bear in ministering to the needs of others.

Faith and persistence—sooner or later it pays off.

CHAPTER 3

Our Awesome God

IN MY PREVIOUS book, *Beauty from Ashes: My Story of Grace*, I told about how I became involved in jail ministry. Among my other involvements now, I continue in that ministry and meet with imprisoned ladies on a weekly basis in a local jail.

People are often pessimistic about how lives can be truly changed inside a jail. Many see a jail as merely a hopeless dead end for people who wind up there. But I have come to love seeing what God does inside prison walls. To me, that place now seems to be the perfect atmosphere for producing miracles.

Many of the female inmates to whom I minister have no religious background at all. A lot of them have never even been in a church a day in their lives. But I find that in many instances they come into the church services I conduct in the jail desperate for answers, and they are receptive to what God wants to give to them.

Most of them have tried much of what the world offers in the way of cheap substitutes for peace and happiness, and they have been greatly disappointed. They've found that everything the enemy of our souls tempts us with has left them empty and longing for more. Some of them are at the end of their ropes and feel that they have no purpose, no hope, and no one who really cares.

It's my great honor to show them the love of Jesus, and I never cease to be amazed at just how far God will go to show them He is real.

And it turns out that lacking a religious background is often a good thing in some of their cases. For without certain religious baggage that many people carry with them throughout life, those ladies simply believe the simplicity and truth of the Word of God as it is presented to them.

Without ever having someone limit their expectations of what God can do today—including what God can do for them— they have the kind of childlike faith that is necessary for believing God and receiving miracles.

One day I went into the jail service, and one of my ladies— that's how I refer to them—came into the room crying rivers of tears. I asked Vicky (not her real name) what was wrong, and she began to tell me about her mother as she wept. She told me her mother was her very best friend, and she lay in a hospital bed— kept alive only by life support—teetering on the edge of death.

Vicky's mother is a diabetic with multiple other health problems, and her body just seemed to have shut down. At that point her mother had fallen into a comatose state, and the doctors didn't expect her to live more than forty-eight hours.

Vicky explained that she wasn't allowed to leave the jail to visit her mom in the hospital, and she was terrified that she would never see her mother again.

Knowing how I would feel if it were my own mother who was dying, my heart began to break for Vicky. I began to explain to the ladies that we might not be able to leave the facility and *physically* go to that hospital, but there is definitely *One* who can.

I shared with them how Jesus healed many people from all kinds of diseases and infirmities during His earthly ministry, and I told them, "He still heals today."

I then asked the ladies to gather around Vicky, and we prayed for her mother right there. I asked Jesus to walk into that hospital room, touch her mother, and heal her of every disease.

After praying, Vicky told me she couldn't understand it, but she felt peace that she didn't think she should possess at such a crucial time in her mother's life. We then began to discuss instances in the Bible where Jesus walked into situations and changed the lives of individuals immediately with His healing touch.

I shared several examples of how Jesus healed people, how the disciples continued to believe Jesus for healing even after He ascended into Heaven, and how they, too, saw miracles take place through their own ministries.

We ended the service, and I left for the day. When I returned the following week, Vicky was the first one in the door. But she wasn't crying that time. She had a huge smile on her face, and she was almost yelling, "Miss Donna, Miss Donna, I have something to tell you!"

She continued to share with me that after I left the previous week, she received a phone call from her aunt, who informed her that her mom had been taken off life support. Her aunt relayed to her that her mom was breathing on her own, and she was wide awake.

Vicky was teary-eyed as she continued to talk about it. She said, "I believe Jesus walked into that hospital room and woke my mother up. But she still doesn't know anyone, and she can't speak. The doctors fear she may have brain damage. Can we pray again?"

I said, "Oh yes! We can pray again. We will pray for her complete recovery."

Then we all gathered around in a circle again and prayed that God would continue the healing process He had started in her mother's body. We all rejoiced in the huge miracle God had already performed, but Vicky wanted *all of her mom back*—not just her physical body but her mental awareness as well.

Vicky came running through the door when I returned the next week. She was so excited to tell me that she had a phone conversation with her mother, and her mother knew her and was able to speak with no problems.

She said, "Miss Donna, I know it had to be God. I thought I would never see my mom again, and now they are saying she will recover enough to go into a nursing home!"

We all rejoiced because of the miraculous intervention of our awesome God. And I inwardly rejoiced specifically because God was revealing himself to those ladies as *their Healer*. In time, Vicky's mother made a full recovery and was allowed to go back to her own home—not the nursing home.

And God was only getting started.

A few weeks later on another of my visits to the jail, Vicky came into the room with tears in her eyes, and she had her hand over her mouth. I almost panicked, hoping that she hadn't received bad news from her mother.

When she sat down at the table, I asked, "Vicky, what is wrong?"

She told me she had an abscessed tooth, and the pain was so intense that she had to cover her mouth because if the air hit her tooth it was almost more than she could bear.

I said, "Vicky, you surely haven't forgotten what God did for your mother have you?"

She said, "No ma'am!"

I asked the other ladies to join me and put their hands on Vicky's shoulders. I placed my hand over Vicky's mouth and began to pray that God would heal her tooth and take away the pain in Jesus' name.

Vicky looked at me with a bewildered expression and said, "Miss Donna, I have goosebumps from my head to my toes! My tooth immediately stopped hurting. I have no pain at all. Thank you, thank you!"

I quickly told her not to thank me, because Jesus was the one who had healed her. I said, "Thank Jesus, He is your Healer."

At that point Vicky had not yet made a commitment to Christ. I was a little surprised that she hadn't already done that after having witnessed all He had done in her life. I couldn't understand why she was hesitating. Still, she said, "Thank You Jesus for healing my mom and my tooth."

Immediately after she said that, another lady spoke up and said, "Miss Donna, my shoulder has been hurting really bad. Would you pray for me?" (We'll call her Tracy.)

Tracy had been coming to the jail church services for quite a while, and I could see how God was moving in her life. She had been seeking Him, and she had been baptized in the Holy Spirit as evidenced by speaking in tongues.

I had witnessed a lot of growth in her as she continued to draw close to God. So I said, "Yes Tracy, I will pray for you on one condition. You have to pray for my shoulder next."

I explained to her that I had been having the same kind of pain in my shoulder for months, and it just wouldn't go away. (And I began to wonder why I had put up with it for so long.)

We gathered around Tracy and began to pray that God would heal her shoulder. I asked her if she could raise her arm. She did! She was thrilled that God had healed her shoulder, and we all continued to rejoice in His miraculous healing power.

Then I said, "Ok, Tracy, it's your turn. I want you to pray for me."

Tracy looked at me like I was crazy, but the ladies all gathered around me, and she began to pray.

I will tell you this: the power and the anointing of the Holy Spirit was evident all over her as she prayed. The presence of the Holy Spirit felt tangible in that sweet moment.

After she finished praying for me, I raised my arm. My shoulder was completely healed too! The pain was gone, and I had full motion once again. I was thrilled as I joyfully told the ladies my shoulder was healed.

As soon as I said those words, Tracy fell on my chest crying like a baby. I said, "Tracy, Tracy, what's wrong?"

She looked at me with tears streaming down her face and said, "Miss Donna, I knew Jesus would answer *your* prayers, but I never dreamed He would actually answer *mine*."

She continued to weep tears of joy, and I did too. I then understood why I had waited so long to ask God to heal my shoulder.

I explained to the ladies that God is no respecter of persons. I told them that healing does not require a well-known healing evangelist, or a high-profile pastor. And I told them Jesus doesn't require us to have all the answers in the world and know every Scripture in the Bible before we pray and have God hear us.

God doesn't maintain a long list of qualifications that have to be checked off before He uses us. He actually *wants* to use us!

We just need to give ourselves to Him and believe it. If we read (educate ourselves) about all that Jesus has done and simply believe that He *still does* what He has always done, we can expect to see miracles in response to our prayers.

I think so many times we get in our own way when it comes to exercising our faith. If we're not careful we start to believe that we need to be in the presence of a great healing minister, or we believe we need to possess a tremendous amount of faith to see God heal and perform miracles. But Jesus said we only need faith as large as a mustard seed.[9]

That's pretty small.

The way I see it, we must simply have childlike faith in the awesome power of our heavenly Father. If we will believe when we pray, He will respond to us. And we will receive miracles.

---

9 "He replied, . . . Truly I tell you, if you have faith as small as a mustard seed, you can say to this mountain, 'Move from here to there,' and it will move. Nothing will be impossible for you" (Matthew 17:20).

We serve an awesome God, and He has not changed. Somewhere along the way, though, *we may have.*

How many of us feel like Tracy? Do we expect to see God do miraculous things through others, but not through us? But why? After all, God is the healer, not us. We're just carrying His message and being His hands and feet.

Vicky was soon to be released from prison, and as I shared earlier, she had not yet made a decision for Christ. She had not come to trust Jesus for salvation even though she had been in the jail for a long time and had attended many of our services. But in the very last service before she was released, she raised her hand and asked for prayer.

I'm thrilled to say that Vicky repented of all her sins that day and accepted Christ as her Savior.

I met Vicky for lunch one day after she was released, and we were finally able to discuss some things privately. I asked her why she had waited so long to come to Jesus after seeing all the miraculous things He was doing in her life.

She said, "Miss Donna, I wanted to make sure I was going to commit. After all God has done, I didn't want to make a commitment and fail Him.

"I wanted to be sure I was ready to walk away from my previous lifestyle and follow Him. But after witnessing all the miracles, I finally knew I could never go back to ordinary. If He was willing to do all those things for me while I was still a sinner, how could I not come to love Him and surrender to Him?"

I never cease to be amazed by how God works in the hearts of the women to whom I minister. God's ways are truly wonderful.

We live in a world that needs to see how wonderful God is. People today are frankly tired of the lip service they often hear among the church crowd when it comes to believing in a God who can change things. They desperately want to see *real* change. They want to see evidence of God's existence and power.

People are living in a world of gloom and fear, and they desperately hope to see something different, something out of the ordinary. They long to see God move in power and know that what they are witnessing is real.

God desires to show himself powerful to such desperate people. But we must believe in Him to do just that. And we must simply believe and allow Him to do that through us.

As time goes on, we continue to see God do miraculous things in the jail. Women have come to Jesus (the greatest miracle of all). And He has healed neck pain, toothaches, headaches, and other ailments.

More and more, the jail ladies simply believe in Jesus to heal their bodies. And they have even learned that it's not necessary for me to be there for them to pray for and receive miracles.

I'm always filled with expectation when I arrive at the jail for our weekly jail service. When I hear about the miracles God performed for my ladies while I was away, I'm especially renewed in my faith and filled with excitement as I continue to proclaim what an *Awesome God* we serve!

CHAPTER 4

Whole in Every Way

IN AN EARLIER chapter, I mentioned my husband sending me to a nice little cabin in Georgia to work on this book. I'm still reaping benefits from that trip. I know without a doubt that God ordered my steps when I ventured off to what I considered to be the *middle of nowhere.*

In my mind I had envisioned a week of silence with no social interaction—just time alone to write and focus on my upcoming book. God had other plans, though. I thought the quietness and beauty of nature would provide inspiration for my book, but actually it was the experiences and the people to whom He introduced me on that trip that inspired me to write.

After spending the first few days at the cabin in complete solitude, the cabin owner, Sheila, sent a text message to me to ask if I needed anything. She was coming by as she checked on some of her other rental properties in the area. Thinking a distraction might be good for me, I asked if I could join her.

When we met in person we had no trouble talking—for about

three hours to be exact—and found that we had a lot in common. Sheila texted me again the next day and said she had someone she wanted me to meet, and I agreed to meet her.

Sheila met me at the cabin at six o'clock the following evening, and we went to a very interesting little place—a store called *Uncle Lar's Outpost*. Sheila wanted me to meet her friend, Shannon, the lady who owns and manages the store. When I met Shannon I could sense there was just something special about her.

We sat out on the front porch of the adorable store and began to talk about my favorite topic—Jesus. I was amazed by her testimony. I could not believe all the things she had dealt with in her life.

Seeing that strong, beautiful lady in front of me, I would never have dreamed that she had been through so much. And I was amazed by how she had come out of the trenches of emotional and physical battles so victorious and glowing with the light and love of Christ.

After talking for a little while, she invited me to come back to the *Outpost* in the future and do a book signing for my book—*Beauty from Ashes*. There was no way I could refuse. After all, it would be like going home to visit two sweet sisters when I returned to Georgia for the book signing.

When I arrived at the store that November, I was soon to learn much more about Shannon and how the miraculous power of God had been working in her life. As she began to share with me a miracle involving her son, neither of us were aware of the miracle God still had in store. We could not have imagined how things would all unfold, and are still unfolding, following our meeting.

Shannon and I were there at Uncle Lar's Outpost as she began to tell me about her childhood.

Shannon was only a young girl when she lost her mother and unborn sister when her mother committed suicide. Shannon later became a ward of the state. At the age of seventeen she was placed in a foster home.

She was happy in her foster home, and she thought the foster family loved her. However, when she turned eighteen her foster parents received their last foster care check from the state for Shannon's care, kicked her out of their home, and had nothing else to do with her.

Three days after her high school graduation, Shannon's only belongings were a car and two dollars. Having no job and no home, she spent the next three days at a roadside rest area.

In desperation she headed to the nearest town and was quickly befriended by those who many people would consider *bad company*—drunks, prostitutes, and bartenders. She was eventually hired to run an after-hours tavern and substitute as a dancer for a local strip club when they needed a fill-in.

Her new friends taught Shannon how to do laundry, shop, pay bills, budget, and save for her own place. According to Shannon, they soon became *the family she never had*. A year later, she was settled into her first apartment, held a real job, paid her own bills, owned a car, and had a boyfriend. Then Shannon decided she wanted a baby—a baby she could love, and who would love her in return.

Shannon said, "Rational, normal influence and guidance was only an afterthought. I was *grown* and wanted a baby, and nothing or no one could stop me."

Shannon soon got what she wished for, and before long she was headed to a hospital delivery room to give birth to a son.

Shannon told me she could still remember the moment of his birth. Her eyes examined every inch of his tiny, perfect body. The delivery room was busy with the hustle and bustle of the nurses and doctor, but there was an absence of one important sound: her precious baby never cried.

She wasn't too worried, though. She just assumed she had the happiest, most content baby ever born.

In the next couple of days, however, after a myriad of tests the doctors informed Shannon that her baby boy had been born deaf.

Shannon's heart dropped in disbelief. Her baby, her tiny child she had so desperately longed for, would never be able to hear his own mother's voice. Crying uncontrollably, Shannon began to question why that had happened to her and her baby.

Mentally scanning through the events leading up to her pregnancy and the delivery, Shannon recalled her frustration as she went to the health department each month to have them administer the test to see if she was pregnant. Three months in a row they told her she was not pregnant. Devastated by the unhappy news each month, Shannon went out and drank and used marijuana to dull the pain she felt.

Then the next month she went to the health department and found out that she was indeed pregnant—three months pregnant!

Remembering her attempts to deal with her disappointment the previous months by drinking and using drugs, Shannon was terrified. She knew that after they told her she wasn't pregnant the previous month she had gone out and not only drank but also dropped acid.[10]

Consumed by guilt and shame—convinced that her drug abuse had caused her son to be deaf—heartbroken, and feeling as if she could not even breathe, Shannon burst into tears. In her mind, she had ruined her son's life. Looking at the tiny child she had so desperately wanted, she felt that she had permanently damaged him.

Feeling like a failure, and while knowing nothing at all about spiritual matters, she recalled that her boyfriend's parents attended a small Pentecostal church. She had no idea what *Pentecostal* was, but her boyfriend's parents continually told her about a man named Jesus, and how God could make things better. Shannon eventually decided to go to the little church with them one day to see what it was all about.

Shannon told me it was a one-room church, and about thirty people were in attendance in the service she visited. She didn't know the people, and she had only been briefly introduced to the pastor. She said she didn't understand what they were talking

---

10 *Drop acid* is common slang for taking LSD (lysergic acid diethylamide). LSD is a potent hallucinogen. Its illicit use was popularized during the 1960s. Birth defects have been attributed to LSD use, but some studies have been inconclusive in proving that. There is a stronger link between LSD and premature birth. However, a stronger link exists between alcohol use by an expectant mother and birth defects. It is common for drug abusers to also be abusers of alcohol, and the combined use of both alcohol and drugs during pregnancy are understood to increase even more the possibility of birth defects and other complications with birth.

about in the service, and she definitely didn't understand anything about God.

But near the end of the service the pastor asked if anyone wanted prayer and instructed those who did to come forward. Shannon grabbed her baby and darted to the altar with tears streaming down her cheeks.

This is the account of what happened next in Shannon's own words:

The pastor asked the rest of the church to come up front and gather in a circle as they began to pray. The pastor then led the prayer, and within minutes everyone was praying. Some prayed softly with their own words, and some began speaking in languages I didn't know.

I had no idea what was happening as I stood in the circle embracing my baby as tightly as I could.

As tears soaked my face and dripped onto my baby's blankets, a man I had never seen before began speaking in tongues—something that always terrified me. I was always taught that speaking in tongues was of the devil and to stay away from it. But I couldn't leave. I wanted my baby to be better!

Soon a lady began speaking directly to me. Her voice was strong and steady, and though I was still nervous, I was strangely calm. I can remember each word as if she just said it to me. It was as if each word became branded inside my heart the moment she spoke it.

She said, "My child, my child, I've seen your tears, and I've heard your weeping. Have no fear, for your child is whole in every way."

She repeated it word for word three times and ended it with, "Your son will do a great work for me, and so shall you."

Immediately the pastor clapped his hands and shouted "HALLELUJAH" as loud as I have ever heard a preacher yell.

My son jolted as if lightning had struck his little body, and he began screaming at the top of his lungs. He screamed so loudly that I was unsure of what was happening or what I should do, but I knew that was the first sound he ever heard.

Watching my son experience deafness, and then witnessing him receive divine healing is extremely hard to explain, but it was one of the most powerful displays of God's divine love I have ever witnessed.

After her baby boy's healing, Shannon still only half-heartedly believed in God and had no concept of what it meant to actually walk with God. She married her son's father, but they divorced when the boy was only seven.

As the boy grew he watched Shannon and his father choose lifestyles of alcohol and drug abuse. Being exposed to a lifestyle of drinking, drugs, unfaithfulness, cheating, and lying became commonplace. And by the age of twelve, Shannon's son began to drink, use marijuana, and accompany his father to local taverns.

"As if that wasn't enough," Shannon told me, "he watched me, his dad, and his stepparents come to Jesus and live out the *church life* for short periods of our lives, only to watch us slip back into our common, familiar, old lifestyles again. It was like being stuck on a broken-down carnival ride."

Shannon married again—and was divorced again. She said that after her second divorce she began to notice her son entering into all kinds of unhealthy relationships, seemingly following in her own footsteps.

By that time Shannon was a mother of three, and she told me it was then that it was as if one day she came to her senses.

She began to see herself as she truly was—the good, the bad, and the ugly. And she saw her own failures reflected especially in the life of her oldest son. She felt as though she had failed miserably as a mother—teaching her children to use and deal drugs, and to live their own lives as full-blown drug addicts.

Shannon decided she had to do something.

Leaving her home in Ohio, Shannon and her two younger children moved to Georgia to start all over. She began attending church again and rededicated her life to Jesus. And for once she wasn't seeking a position in the church, special recognition, or even a pat on the back. She just wanted to live a better life and to live it for the Lord.

She hoped to become a living testimony to her children. She wanted to show them that God was and is real. Shannon told me it was incredibly hard because she was facing a mountain of guilt.

The "should haves, would haves, and could haves" tormented her daily for the first few years of her new life in Christ.

But eventually a few years turned into five years, and ten years, and then fifteen years of walking faithfully with Jesus.

Then with Shannon's two younger children living for Jesus as well, she was especially tormented because her oldest son was still far from Christ.

It had been thirty-five years since her son had received his miracle of divine healing, and Shannon was still waiting for all of God's promise to her to be fulfilled. The entire word she received all those years ago was that her son would be whole in *every* way and do a great work for God.

And he was still lost in sin.

If I had written this chapter right after returning to Uncle Lar's Outpost for the book signing, this is where the story would have concluded. It would have been a wonderful testimony to the miraculous power of God—how He instantly healed that precious baby boy all those years ago, and how God finally worked miracles of redemption and restoration in Shannon's life.

But the story was far from over.

When I returned to Georgia for the book signing, Shannon was still waiting for all of her miracle. Being with her again and talking more with her was inspiring. I was so amazed by how tightly Shannon held on to the promise of God even though it seemed her son was straying farther from God than he ever had in the past.

With a family and children of his own, her son was living a life of misery and raising his own children to follow in his footsteps.

Shannon went to Ohio to visit with him not long after I left Georgia the second time. And she recently corresponded with me to tell me the rest of the story that I relate to you below:

She told me she was so heartbroken after spending time in Ohio with her son and her grandchildren that she cried most of the way home. Her grandchildren knew nothing about God, and they had no desire to go to church. Her son's life was completely out of control, and his marriage was destined for disaster.

But Shannon realized she wasn't just upset because her son was still so lost; she was sick and tired of the enemy having his way with her family. And she was ready to see the total fulfillment of God's promise.

Shannon determined it was time to go to war. When she returned home she talked to her two younger children and told them it was time to fight for her son—their brother. The three of them agreed to fast and pray for seven days and ask God to intervene and do whatever it took to see her lost son come to Christ.

Shannon began to quote Scriptures containing the promises of God, and she fortified herself with the promises God had made to her concerning her son. Shannon and her two—now grown—children surrounded her son with prayer by taking shifts around the clock to lift him before the heavenly Father.

They asked God to do whatever it took to break him and turn his heart to Jesus.

Three weeks later Shannon received a phone call from her son. Shannon said he was broken, crying, and sobbing harder than she had ever heard him before. He told her he had found out his wife was in the middle of an affair, and he didn't know what to do.

Shannon felt that the breaking process had begun. She asked God to guard her heart and her words, and help her to stay out of the Holy Spirit's way.

A week later Shannon's son called again to tell her that he had gone to church and surrendered his life to Christ. He told her he did not want to keep living his life the way he had been.

Shannon told me it was the first time in fifteen years that her son had attempted to live a sober life on a daily basis. God was transforming him day by day as the Lord surrounded him with loving, caring Christians who were encouraging him. And his pastor called him multiple times a day and poured into him.

God certainly answered their prayers and sent reinforcements to help rescue Shannon's son.

Shannon wrote:

My son's life has now turned around. He not only was introduced to Jesus, but he chooses to follow Jesus and be a partner with Him in this life he was given. He is sharing Jesus with all those around him.

The greatest testimony he shares is not simply the story of his healing as a baby; the greatest impact is when his words are matched by the demonstration of his life-choices and how he conducts his daily life now. He's living his testimony. This is the fulfillment of the miracle God spoke over my son the day his ears began to work!

Thirty-five years later, I am privileged to see my God performing all He has promised. I see all of my children and grandchildren attending church services—delighted to participate and learn. I see them learning Scriptures and bowing their little heads to pray over the food as they give thanks to God for all His blessings.

I see my son sharing the good news of all Jesus has done in his life as his children ask questions and begin to serve Jesus too! God has truly made my son whole in every way.

As I think back over the conversations Shannon and I had at the Outpost, I'm impressed with her determination to see every word the Father promised come to pass. She has now seen two amazing miracles in her son's life. One was the miraculous healing he received as a baby. The other was his miraculous redemption and spiritual transformation experienced so many years later.

Many years ago a woman yielded her vocal chords to God while part of a group of believers circled around praying for a baby born deaf. The Lord spoke through her and told the baby's mother the child would be "whole in every way." Actually, His words were "your child *is* whole in every way."

As far as God was concerned (using His words), all that God has now done for the child—and for the grown man the child became—was an established fact from the beginning. It was determined. It was done in heaven.

It was true in heaven, and it was inevitable that God's words would also eventually be proven true on earth as the child's mother and others continued to hold on to God's promise, believe, and trust in God and His Word for miracles.

God is not just unlimited in His power, He is also unlimited when it comes to time. Time limits us, but it doesn't limit God. When Peter wrote about patiently trusting in and waiting for the Lord's return, he said:

> *But do not forget this one thing, dear friends: With the Lord a day is like a thousand years, and a thousand years are like a day.* (2 Peter 3:8)

Time limits us, and we often struggle with it. It sometimes stresses us and causes us much grief. But God is ultimately in control of all time, so when it comes to God's promises, they are sure to come to pass regardless of how much time we need to wait for them. We can have confidence in that.

In time, just in time, God will act and do miraculous things to amaze us.

We rejoice in the works and faithfulness of God. We revel in and give Him praise for all the miracles He has performed and continues to perform daily.

There are good reasons for us to be especially impressed with and be thankful for miracles of healing. But we must acknowledge that until we have accepted Christ as our Savior, none of us are *whole in every way.*

CHAPTER 5

Miracles of Provision

THERE IS NO doubt that we serve a miracle-working God. He delights in blessing us with miracles of healing, intervention, protection, and so much more. God is our protector and our healer. But God is also *our Provider*, and He often provides for us in miraculous ways.

There are so many instances in the Bible where we read of how God miraculously provided for His children. In fact there are too many to list, so I'm just going to quickly mention a few and move on.

God provided for the children of Israel as they wandered in the wilderness for forty years. Not only did He provide food and water for them, He even sent down manna from heaven to feed them.[11] And though they traveled for forty years, their clothes

---

11 God miraculously provided the Israelites water from the rocks on two occasions (Exodus 17:1-7 and Numbers 20:1-13). He also healed the bitter waters of Marah for them in the Desert of Shur so the water would be fit for the Israelites to drink (Exodus 15:22-26). And for food, God not only gave the Israelites manna to gather in the morning but also on more than one occasion gave them quail to eat (Exodus 16:1-13, Numbers 11:4-32,

and sandals never wore out.[12]

I've done well to own a pair of shoes for four years. Four years is a miracle in my case.

We've also read about Jesus feeding over five thousand people with two small fishes and five loaves of bread.[13] There's also the instance when Jesus told Peter to go and catch a fish, and in its mouth he would find a four-drachma coin to pay their temple taxes.[14]

I would like to get my tax money from a fish. I would certainly do more fishing.

God loves to provide for His children. And He has promised to supply all our needs.[15] But sometimes He provides things for us that would not be classified as "needs" just to show us His affection.

I was traveling one Saturday to speak at a church on Sunday morning, and for some reason I started thinking about coconut

---

and Psalm 105:40). As for God feeding the Israelites for forty years with manna, that was such a significant and unique miracle that there is no other occurrence in the biblical record or modern history of God using manna to feed people again.

"The Israelites ate manna forty years, until they came to a land that was settled; they ate manna until they reached the border of Canaan" (Exodus 16:35).

12 "Yet the LORD says, "During the forty years that I led you through the wilderness, your clothes did not wear out, nor did the sandals on your feet" (Deuteronomy 29:5).

13 Matthew 14:14-21.

14 Matthew 17:24-27.

15 "And my God will meet all your needs according to the riches of his glory in Christ Jesus" (Philippians 4:19). Read also Luke 12:22-34.

cream pie. I was thinking about how nice it would be to have a great big piece of coconut cream pie. I didn't mention it to anyone. It was just a thought or perhaps a craving I had.

When the church service was over that Sunday morning, a lady approached me and said, "I know this is a crazy question, but do you like coconut cream pie?"

I said, "Yes, I certainly do!"

She said, "Well, okay. You are the one I'm supposed to give it to. Last night when I was at home God told me to make a coconut cream pie and take it to church with me the next morning. He said He would show me who to give it to."

It wasn't that I *needed* the coconut cream pie, and heaven knows I certainly didn't need the calories. I was so blessed to find out that the very day I was thinking I would like a piece of coconut cream pie, God was putting it on someone's heart to make one for me. That is just like our God. He loves us and delights in us.

And it shows.

God loves to bless us. He provides for us in many ways—in big ways and in small ways as well—and all of His miraculous provisions demonstrate His love and prove the reality of His interest in our lives.

I have always given books that I have written to the ladies I minister to in jail. They love having reading material. But it can get very expensive to give away books every week. One day after our church service in the jail, the ladies asked if I had any other books that I could bring for them. I told them I would try to look into it that week.

I didn't mention it to anyone else. It was just a conversation that I had with the ladies in the jail. That very same day, though, one of my pastor-friends, who is also an author, contacted me and told me that he would like to donate two cases of his latest book to my jail ministry.

He had no idea that I would be looking for books that week. God put it on his heart to donate two cases of books to me. He obeyed, and my need—and that of the jail ladies—was met.

I experienced a similar situation when the ladies in the jail needed thermal undergarments because of the cold temperatures in the prison.

I traveled to another state to speak at a women's event at a church. When I arrived I was amazed to find that the ladies of the church had purchased thermal underwear for my jail ladies and brought them to the speaking event to give to me. Once again, another need was met in a clearly miraculous way.

God is a loving Father to us, and as such, He desires to provide for our needs. An interest in providing for his children is one of the characteristics of any good father. A good father wants to make sure his children are well taken care of.

God is *Jehovah Jireh,* which means *the Lord will provide.*[16] The Lord is our provider, and He delights in providing for and taking care of His children.

In all three of my personal examples above, God demonstrated that He was going before me and providing for me and others even before I mentioned a need to either Him or anyone else. I didn't have to pray and ask Him to provide, He just did it.

---

16 YHWH-Yireh—Yahweh provides. This is one of several names through which the Lord's person is revealed by His actions as recorded in the Bible. Jehovah Jireh (or spelled Jehovah-jireh) comes from only one passage in Scripture—the account of God providing for Abraham a ram for sacrifice. (Genesis 22:13-14).

Sometimes God chooses to bless us in that way. I think He does so to help us realize that He knows our needs before we even mention them.

> *And when you pray, do not keep on babbling like pagans, for they think they will be heard because of their many words. Do not be like them, for your Father knows what you need before you ask him.* (Matthew 6:7-8)

Jesus encouraged His followers to pray, but He also encouraged them to understand that our heavenly Father knows all things and has good ears.

It encourages us to know that, even before we ask, God is already aware of what's going on in our lives and wants to provide for even our smallest needs—and many times our smallest desires.

Of course there are other times when God purposely withholds things from us until we go to Him and ask for them.

> *You desire but do not have, so you kill. You covet but you cannot get what you want, so you quarrel and fight. You do not have because you do not ask God.* (James 4:2)

In his words of correction, James includes the thought that instead of people presenting their needs to God and wisely waiting for God to provide solutions to them, they too often go about pursuing things in their own ways. And instead of receiving God's intended provisions, their ways of pursuing what they want without God's direction and involvement can lead to terrible actions and spiritual ruin.

As we learn from and respond to this Scripture passage from the book of James, we need to recognize that James went on to say that there is another reason people sometimes don't receive what they want. That is, they don't ask for the right reason—they have the wrong motives.[17] But right now we'll continue to focus on the topic of not asking God. I have more to say about our motives in chapter nine.

God wants us to admit our needs, take them to Him, and then depend on Him to provide for us in the right way and for the right reasons.

Recognizing our own needs, and recognizing God as the source of our sustenance, is good for us. Clearly we learn from both Scripture and personal experience that God wants us to remember who our lives truly depend on. And yet when faced with a significant need, many of us will go to the ends of the earth to find an answer before we ever ask Jesus to help us.

I admit that I've been guilty of doing that at times, myself.

When faced with problems, many of us feel like we can and should fix or change our situations through our own human efforts. We often exhaust all of our earthly options first and then, as a last resort, ask God to help us.

Can you imagine how we must appear to God when we do that? And we might run ourselves ragged to come up with a solution to a problem, while God has already provided the perfect answer and is just waiting to release it when we ask Him.

---

17 "When you ask, you do not receive, because you ask with wrong motives, that you may spend what you get on your pleasures" (James 4:3).

When my husband, Bryan, was promoted to a management position in 2006, one of the requirements of being given the position was that he would agree to be assigned to a different facility in a different state. According to the plan, after finishing the three-year-long assignment, we could move back to Tennessee if there was an opening at that facility.

He soon accepted a position in Iowa.

We needed to sell our home as soon as possible and move immediately. We had not lived in our current home in Tennessee very long—only a couple of years. Before we bought the house, it had been listed with two different realtors for over a year without any sincere interest or offers from anyone. So when we decided to purchase it back then, we bought the house at a greatly reduced price.

Then when it came time for us to have to sell that house, we were afraid it would take a very long time again for it to sell because of the current market, and because we knew people were not interested in the house before we bought it.

We began to pray that God would help us to sell the house quickly.

We had just set up an appointment with a realtor for the purpose of listing our house for us when we received a telephone call from another realtor from another real estate agency. She told us that a couple she represented as agent had driven by our house and thought our home would be perfect for their needs. They wondered if we would be interested in selling, so they asked the realtor if she would contact us to see if we might have a desire to sell.

Being suspicious, I first thought that realtor had heard through the grapevine we were planning to sell and was simply hoping for a chance to list the house for us. I told her we had agreed to sign a contract with another realtor. I assumed we would never hear from her again. But the ink wasn't even dry on the paperwork with our realtor before she called our agent and arranged a showing.

We were literally sitting at the table signing the papers with our realtor when she called!

The people wanted to see the house immediately—before it could even be publicly listed—and insisted on seeing it the very next day, which was Sunday. We went to church that morning and stayed away from our home long enough for the couple to tour the house.

To our surprise, our realtor called and told us that when we arrived home we would find a signed contract on the kitchen table with an offer to buy our house at full-asking-price.

We had listed our house with plenty of room to come down if it didn't sell immediately. Yet there was an offer on the table for the initial asking price! There was no haggling or counter offers. Our home was sold, and we were free to begin our search for a new home in Iowa.

We were amazed to find the perfect home in the perfect location in Iowa, and we were moved into it before Bryan even reported to work the first day. That was considered to be impossible by many people he worked with. But our God is the God of miracles!

That would have been a great ending to the story, but it doesn't end there. Nine years later God revealed to us clearly, in a significant way, that it was time to move back to Tennessee. Once again we had to sell our home immediately.

It was a terrible time to buy or sell a house because the economy was not doing well, especially in our area. Many large employers had shut down, and many people were looking for *jobs*—not large homes to buy.

When we listed our house the realtor told us that she didn't want to discourage us, but houses in our area—and in our home's price range—were simply not selling. She told us her house was the same size as ours, in the same price range as ours, newer and more modern, and it had been on the market for over three years.

Seemingly facing impossible odds, we began to pray. And believe it or not, before our realtor could even get the photos of our home uploaded onto the real estate website, we had three couples requesting to see our home.

The first couple to see it made an offer contingent on the sale of their home. The second couple made an offer to purchase immediately at the asking price. And the third couple made an offer above the asking price to purchase it immediately and take possession before the end of the month!

Once again we experienced a miracle of God's provision. There could be no other explanation.

Again God answered our prayers in a way that amazed us. And that time He didn't just prepare and send a buyer to us at just the right time, He even sent back-up buyers! He is faithful to answer, and it's always best when we go to Him first instead of trying to take matters into our own hands.

Our heavenly Father knows no boundaries when it comes to taking care of His own. Bad economies, insufficient numbers of buyers in the marketplace, and any other impossible situations that end the plans of others cannot stop the Lord from answering our prayers and meeting our needs.

He has no limits!

God blesses us many times by doing things for us just to show us His love. And the Lord responds over and over to meet our needs when we present them to Him in prayer. But there are other times when He also blesses us according to our obedience and faithfulness.

My parents have repeatedly reminded me of a situation they faced when my brother and I were small children. My parents both held good, steady jobs and had respectable incomes. The time came when they decided to build a new house. And they also purchased a new car at the same time. But after making those purchases, situations changed.

Only weeks after moving into the new house, both of my parents were laid off from their jobs. They were struggling to survive on a total income of one hundred dollars a week. Christmas was only weeks away. And my parents were devastated at the thought of not being able to buy gifts or provide any kind of Christmas excitement that year for my brother and me.

Yet because they believed God was faithful, and they were just as obedient to Him in paying their tithes on their one-hundred-dollar income as they were with their previous, much more considerable income, God provided them with a miracle.

One day one of my dad's friends asked him to go to a music

store with him to look for an organ to buy for his wife for Christmas. The music store owners were hosting a big giveaway and were asking everyone to sign up. My dad and his friend both put their names and addresses into the box.

The odds of winning were very small, and neither of them afterward gave it a second thought.

A few days later, though, my dad received a telephone call to inform him that he had won the drawing. To his surprise the reward included the payment of all bills for that month plus five hundred dollars cash.

God miraculously provided for my parents that Christmas season, and He continued to provide for our family in amazing ways until my parents were both working again.

My parents taught my brother and me with an illustration that we could not ignore. When people choose to put God first in everything—especially in tithing on their income—He in turn never fails to provide for them and bless them for their obedience and faithfulness.

God certainly doesn't need our money. He owns the cattle on a thousand hills,[18] and that's just the beginning. But He rewards those who are faithful and obedient to Him, and He is mindful of the desperate times in which they sometimes live.

My parents could have considered holding on to every penny of their insufficient income in an attempt to stretch it. But they trusted God. They knew He was able to take what was left over

---

18 "Listen, my people, and I will speak; I will testify against you, Israel: I am God, your God. . . . I have no need of a bull from your stall or of goats from your pens, for every animal of the forest is mine, and the cattle on a thousand hills" (Psalm 50:7-10).

after paying their tithes and miraculously multiply it to meet their needs, and that is exactly what He did.

When we are faithful with what God has given us, He is faithful to honor that and provide for our needs.

Like I have said many times, God is a good Father! He not only understands our needs but also is interested in supplying them. He longs to provide for us, and He often provides for us in miraculous, unexpected ways. And if we're observant we will recognize that.

No boundaries exist when it comes to God's abilities to bless and provide for His children. We must always remember that we have a provider in heaven who knows our needs and knows no limits. That will increase our faith and give us confidence to trust Him every day.

And as we pray and present our requests to the Lord with our faith and confidence in Him strong and immoveable, we will stop being headstrong and guilty of trying to work out our problems or pursue our desires in our own strength. We will rely on God to supply all our needs.

We will be quick to run to our *Daddy* in heaven—our miraculous provider!

CHAPTER 6

Perils of Fanaticism

WHEN IT COMES to my preaching, anyone who has ever heard me speak would most likely say that I have a quiet demeanor.

I'm not one to yell, shout, or jump over pews. I don't run up and down the aisles or drag people to the altar. I don't tend to scream out like a wild banshee or yell loud enough to wake the dead (this statement will find more context later). I typically speak in a very conversational manner.

Although I seldom see a minister jump over a pew, many of them are more emotional in their deliveries than I am. And I have to admit that I've sometimes felt intimidated by other ministers who are extremely vocal and much more animated than I.

Because of my style of delivery I've often felt that listeners might not think I was as well equipped to preach like the more demonstrative preachers.

I used to ask God to make me bolder and louder. He hasn't changed me yet, though, and I now think He probably won't. I've come to understand that God not only uses us and empowers us through the Holy Spirit as unique individuals but also uses our own personalities to benefit the Kingdom in the way He chooses.

My personality has always been quiet and conversational. And God uses me and my quiet, conversational ways.

Some ministers speak loudly and are much more animated in their ministries. That is their personality, and that is fine with me as long as they are sincere and wisely doing God's bidding. I've come to understand that different preachers minister in different ways, and God uses all types to reach people with the miraculous Gospel of Jesus Christ.

In the end, it's not our particular *style* of preaching that makes the difference. What matters most is that the preacher is truly following the direction of the Holy Spirit.

When dealing with, ministering in, and living in the realm of the miraculous, it is inevitable that sooner or later—regardless of the ministry styles we experience—we are going to be confronted with what is commonly referred to in church circles as *excess*.

Many people are turned off by the excess they see and decide to avoid participating in anything to do with the miraculous. And sometimes the views they develop against excess even drive them to mistakenly oppose and fight against beliefs in divine healing and the working of miracles.

God lives in the realm of the miraculous and wants us to benefit from His power to save, heal, deliver, and do all the other things He does in working miracles among us. So it would be a mistake for us to attempt to appease naysayers by backing off our message.

We must continue speaking truth and spreading the Good News that *"Jesus Christ is the same yesterday and today and forever."*[19]

But we can and should be willing to recognize and deal with excess.

I've traveled a lot in my life and ministry. I've been a lot of places—churches, conference venues, and other places of ministry. I have heard many preachers speak. And as I've experienced their ministries over the years I have sometimes seen some *unusual* things.

Some of those things have bothered me little. Some have bothered me a lot. But there is nothing that has bothered me more than when I witness what I believe to be fanaticism.

A *fanatic* is defined as "a person with an extreme and uncritical enthusiasm or zeal, as in religion or politics."[20]

As I describe it, extreme in this context refers to behavior that is *over the top*. It's too much, uncalled for, unnecessary, and unbecoming. And being *uncritical* centers around not being able to control or judge our own behavior when it comes to what is acceptable or suitable.

Two synonyms for *uncritical* are *shallow* and *superficial.*[21]

Fanaticism by any definition has to do with excessive or irrational behavior. And of course to handle fanaticism honestly we must admit that even though fanaticism is a clearly defined thing, how it is judged is somewhat up to the people doing the judging. (But ultimately of course it's up to God.)

We Pentecostals are often labeled fanatical by non-Pentecostals. And we'll respond to them by pointing to Scriptures

---

19 Hebrews 13:8.
20 https://www.dictionary.com/browse/fanatic
21 https://www.dictionary.com/browse/uncritical

to prove them wrong. Hopefully we Pentecostals also will rely on the Scriptures to back up our own views of what is fanatical.

Therefore, my brothers and sisters, be eager to prophesy, and do not forbid speaking in tongues. But everything should be done in a fitting and orderly way. (1 Corinthians 14:39-40)

I was born about the time Kathryn Kuhlman died. Perhaps you wouldn't think someone in my generation would think so highly of her and her ministry, but I love to listen to recordings of her preaching and teaching. I have always admired her humility and how God used her to bring miracles of healing to people.

I was recently listening to a recording of one of her messages, and I couldn't have agreed more with a statement she made on the subject of fanaticism.

She said:

A little knowledge and an overabundance of zeal always tends to be harmful, and in the area involving religious truths it can be disastrous, very disastrous.

In our great zeal to do God's work—to make a difference in people's lives—any of us can make the mistake of letting our zeal get ahead of good reason and the wisdom God gives us to help us stay balanced in our faith. We can get in trouble when our zeal rises above godly wisdom.

Unrestrained zeal can cause us to go beyond reason, exceed biblical checks and balances, and lead us into fanatical behavior.

When I think of over-the-top demonstrations in ministry I often think of preachers being caught up in *helping* the Holy Spirit far too much when they are praying for people through the laying on of hands. Many of us have had experiences with an overzealous minister who, while praying for us, tried to push us down so we could be what Pentecostals call *slain in the Spirit.*

Being slain in the Spirit—or *falling under the power*—is an experience that is a little difficult to explain to one who has never experienced it personally. It's a real experience, and it has not always been relegated to Pentecostal or charismatic movements. Falling under the power can be traced back through Church history in various revival movements for hundreds of years in America alone.[22]

Having experienced being slain in the Spirit myself, I can only describe it as being overwhelmed and overcome by the power of God. It's as if God poured so much of His power into me that my physical body simply couldn't contain it. Anytime I have experienced it my legs have felt like *Jello* giving way beneath me and leaving me on the floor.

There is nothing like it when God truly moves in power.

I feel that when people are slain in the Spirit He takes them into a deeper knowledge and understanding of Him. I believe our faith is built as we physically *feel* God's power. For that reason alone there is nothing quite as frustrating to me than feeling a

---

22 http://www.apologeticsindex.org/2924-slain-in-the-spirit. This online opinion statement by David Kowalski, Assemblies of God pastor and Professor for Global University, contains a thoughtful handling of both the history, reality, and sometimes excessive displays of people experiencing the manifestation of *falling under the power.*

minister trying to push me to the floor—or witness it so obviously happen to someone else.

I have seen many people fall under God's power without anyone ever having laid a hand on them. I have myself prayed for others and not even touched them when they suddenly fell to the floor under the power of God. And then I have had ministers who have prayed for me and pushed me so hard that I felt as if I would fall because of their own power—certainly not God's.

To me their unrestrained zeal led them to attempt to orchestrate the activities of the Holy Spirit. That was unwise because such orchestration can lead to counterfeit experiences. And counterfeit experiences all too often lead to the Church and the Holy Spirit earning a bad reputation instead of bringing glory to God.

When the Holy Spirit is in charge of the situation, God does not need our physical help in laying people out on the floor. So yes, I believe a person applying pressure to people's foreheads while praying for them to influence them to yield to the Holy Spirit and *fall under the power* is uncalled for, over-the-top, not wise, and lends itself to fanaticism.[22]

Although there are many Christians who are moved emotionally by fanatical behavior and will accept it—they can't seem to bring themselves to question it[23]—there are others who recognize it for what it is.

---

23 1 Thessalonians 5:19-20 and 1 John 4:1 speaks to the Church testing the *words* of others. 1 Corinthians 5:12-13 speaks to judging *deeds*. People sometimes fear the idea of examining others and holding them accountable in the Church—especially when we talk about leaders. But while Christians must always be respectful and not take such a thing lightly, we actually have a responsibility to judge what is done among us. We are not only to judge between right and wrong when it comes to words but also actions.

Some of those will become disillusioned with ministries. And some of those observing excess will over-react and end up becoming satisfied with lower expectations of our miracle-working Savior. And that is so sad because it is so unnecessary.

And when it comes to non-believers—or those who are skeptical of the power of the Holy Spirit in the first place—they will use fanatical behavior to reinforce their unbelief and teach others that none of what God does in the realm of the miraculous is real.

How tragic. I don't know about you, but I have no desire for any counterfeit manifestation of God.

I want only the *real thing*!

When asked about her healing ministry and how God healed so many in her services, Kathryn Kuhlman told people that it was strange to some because of the fact that hundreds had been healed just sitting quietly in the audience without any physical demonstration whatsoever.

She said:

> Very often, not even a sermon is preached. There have been times when not even a song has been sung. No loud demonstration, no loud calling on God as though He were deaf, no screaming, no manifestations of the flesh, no exhorting, no admonishing, just the very presence of the Holy Spirit.[24]

24 From Kathryn Kuhlman's sermon: *The Secret of Miracles Revealed in Jesus' Life*, recorded by Springs of Living Water Tapes Library, Spring Lake, MN, Audio Published on YouTube by Fruitful Sermons, July 5, 2015.

The Holy Spirit is gentle. Clearly He is extremely powerful, but He normally works softly and certainly needs no help from anyone's loud vocalizations or forceful movements to get His work done. In fact, when there is a real and genuine move of the Holy Spirit, no one has to even be notified of what is happening.

There needn't be a word spoken. People can sense and feel a genuine move of the Spirit. He doesn't need us to work up the audience into a frenzy of excitement.

Most of the time the Holy Spirit just needs us to get out of the way.

The way it appears, it seems to me that some people think they can encourage the miraculous moving of the Holy Spirit by their own actions. And I'm not sure why. God is sovereign. He will do as He desires. We can pray vocally and publicly and ask Him to heal or answer other types of prayers for people, but we don't need to put on a show in the process.

There is nothing to be gained by appearing in any way to manipulate the Holy Spirit.

There is no secret formula for making sure God arrives and backs up our message. There is no dance routine or specific prayer that must be spoken. We simply rely on the Holy Spirit to bring both God's Holy Word and His presence and influence to bear in services where people can receive what God has for them.

Kathryn Kuhlman said she was always sure of two things. One was that she herself had nothing to do with what was happening when people were healed. And the second thing was that God would never share the glory with anyone. According to her (and I agree) both the power and the glory belong to Jesus alone.

The way I see it, that takes a huge amount of pressure off

of me. If I prayed for people while feeling I was the healer, and people didn't receive their healing, then I could easily feel as if I failed them. But knowing that Jesus is the one who heals—having confidence in the fact He chooses when, how, and whom He will heal—helps me to know that it's not about me.

I don't need to feel responsible for doing anything but obediently following the leading of the Holy Spirit. And I don't need to have all the answers when it comes to how and when people are healed.

If I had all the answers and knew why He healed some people and not others, I would be like God. I do not know why He does or doesn't heal, and that makes me human.

I can rest in the fact that God is in control, and I willingly yield to Him all control to do as He chooses.

I was once invited to speak at a two-day women's event where some other ministers were also speaking. I really didn't know what to expect going into it because I didn't know many of the people hosting or attending the event.

The first service started, and when the worship music began there was a sweet presence of the Holy Spirit in the auditorium. We sang several songs, and then, suddenly, a few ladies began to run around the building waving flags and screaming—literally.

It was almost as if the Holy Spirit was ushered out of the building in the following moments.

Some of the ladies had what appeared to be walking sticks, and they were hitting the floor with the sticks as they ran back and forth across the front of the auditorium. My friend who was attending with me looked at me, and I knew she was wondering the same thing I was:

"What on earth is going on here?"

I simply could not worship because of all the commotion— including the fear of having my toes crushed by the *walking sticks* that were coming nearer and nearer to my feet. Then suddenly one of the ladies whizzed by me screaming in my ear as she passed.

She nearly scared me to death.

Clearly, I was still very much alive, but I can't say as much for the *entertainment.* It was completely dead. There was no anointing upon it, and there was no spiritual power in it. The only thing that I could see it producing was a lot of confusion.

My spirit was grieved within me. And I wasn't the only one who felt like that.

The first speaker then took the mic and began to shout, yell, and run back and forth across the platform. She loudly berated— yes, berated—the congregation for what seemed like an hour or two. I was so amazed and taken aback by her strange facial expressions and the wildly animated delivery of her sermon that I can't even tell you what she preached that night.

After observing her delivery, and after seeing all the other things that went on before it, I was certain that the ladies in the auditorium were not going to be at all interested in my quiet and calm demeanor.

By the time my turn came to preach I had come to grips with the thought that I certainly wouldn't be *spiritual enough* by the standards already displayed in the meeting.

But there is something we can always count on. The Holy Spirit is true to himself—always.

Wherever and whenever there are people who need to be ministered to, the Holy Spirit will be there. He cannot be anything but good. He is genuine, and He cannot be imitated (although there are those who try). So the next morning as I anxiously took the platform, I simply and quietly spoke what the Lord had given me for those ladies.

You could almost hear a pin drop. There were no loud "Amens," from the congregation. There was no running or shouting. There was just the quiet and peaceful presence of the Holy Spirit's power.

People immediately came forward for prayer when I gave the altar call. I didn't bring them to the front for prayer because I was loud, because I wasn't. It wasn't because I ran the length of the platform swinging my arms and shouting, because I didn't. The response could only be attributed to me moving out of the way and letting the Holy Spirit do what He was there to do.

I was in awe.

It wasn't my place that day to put on a show and pretend I was the master of ceremonies. It wasn't my responsibility to work the crowd's emotions into a frenzy. My job was to simply speak the words God was giving me and not allow my flesh to get in the way.

The people who responded to the altar call were touched as the Holy Spirit gently moved on them and met their needs. I didn't have to beg anyone to come forward. The Holy Spirit compelled them to come to the altar. It was His work, not mine, and it was beautiful.

People noticed a difference. They could feel the Holy Spirit. They didn't need a spectacular demonstration or a loud demand for them to come forward. They just came because they knew the Holy Spirit was there to minister.

But when the last speaker took the platform she began to mock me. She began to make fun of some of the things I had spoken about. I could not believe it. Then she started pointing at people and giving—or yelling—*prophetic words.*

The Holy Spirit is not rude or insulting. He operates lovingly and wisely in all He does, and I could sense no love or wisdom in what was taking place.[25]

Don't get me wrong, I believe in the prophetic gifts. God uses me prophetically on occasion. But when God gives me words to deliver to someone, I speak them privately to the individual—typically when I am praying for the person. I don't yell at them across the auditorium so everyone else can hear what is being said.

I believe if God has something to say to the group, He will speak to them as a group. But when God chooses to reveal something to an individual person through a prophetic word, I don't believe He intends for people across town to hear it as well. It's not necessary to share with the whole congregation what God intends for one individual.

Perhaps if I felt differently, though, I could attract more attention to my own spirituality and call myself a prophet.

No, I think I will try to resist pride and just be me.

---

25 "Love is patient and kind. Love is not jealous or boastful or proud or rude. It does not demand its own way. It is not irritable, and it keeps no record of being wronged" (1 Corinthians 13:4-5 NLT).

Years ago I worked in a beauty salon, and every week there was a certain lady who came in to get her hair styled.

It never failed that when the lady came into the salon she would start jerking violently and tell everyone that the Holy Spirit had just *hit her*. She would announce to everyone that she needed to go into her *prayer closet* and pray, and she would then retreat to the only restroom in the salon.

When she had locked the door behind her she would begin praying in tongues as loudly as she could. That would go on for at least thirty minutes. People in the salon would begin to look at each other and laugh, or roll their eyes.

Others would ask, "What in the world is she doing?"

That was clearly gross fanaticism on display, and it did nothing to inspire others. It only caused confusion. And it caused frustration and aggravation for those who needed to access the restroom. In that situation, too, I sensed no wisdom in what was being attributed to the Holy Spirit's leading.

Jesus tells us in His Word that we should not flaunt our spirituality and righteous acts in front of people with the intention of drawing attention to ourselves. (And as far as I'm concerned that goes for both prayer and preaching.)

Be careful not to practice your righteousness in front of others
to be seen by them. If you do, you will have no reward from
your Father in heaven. . . . And when you pray, do not be like
the hypocrites, for they love to pray standing in the synagogues

and on the street corners to be seen by others. Truly I tell you, they have received their reward in full.

But when you pray, go into your room, close the door and pray to your Father, who is unseen. Then your Father, who sees **what is done in secret,** *will reward you.*

(Matthew 6:1-6 [emphasis mine])

I found it hard to believe that the woman's prayer room just so happened to be in a beauty salon where everyone could hear her prayers. I believe we must always use wisdom in how we conduct ourselves, or we will destroy our witness.

Other things that border on excess or fanaticism bother me, but I will mention only one more:

I have seen individuals or ministers claim that a miracle, such as a healing, has taken place when nothing happened. People may have good intentions, but when we claim a miracle has happened, and everyone else knows no actual miracle took place, we are yet again doing damage to our witness.

Like me, other people are also looking for the *real thing*.

When it comes to miracles, skeptics will naturally do everything they can to prove they didn't occur. And when it turns out that no actual miracle took place as claimed, the skeptics will be emboldened and certainly make it known. We should not feed their fire with false claims.

Why would we ever want to substitute something fake for the real thing, especially when our God still performs real miracles?

There is no need to try to pass off any kind of imitation as a real move of God initiated by the Holy Spirit.

When we humbly seek God for what He has promised, and when we simply rely on the Holy Spirit's power within us—the same power that raised Christ from the dead—then we can and will see the Holy Spirit reveal God and His power to us and through us in wisdom, in real ways, and in real miracles.

To avoid the perils of fanaticism, we must always keep the focus off of us and our methods. We must seek to do only those things that the Holy Spirit is truly leading us to do. We must avoid shallow and superficial demonstrations that serve to only highlight our own part in ministry and take the glory away from God.

When God is glorified and we seek to humbly lift Him up—resisting our own pride and refusing to fall prey to excessive behavior—others will simply see His miracles and believe in the God we serve.

CHAPTER 7

Never Give Up

WHEN I FIRST started writing the book you are holding—after I felt God wanted me to write an *entire* book centered around the miraculous—I was concerned that I wouldn't have enough material to fill the pages. But I've learned over time to simply start doing the work that God impresses upon me to do and leave the details of how to finish the work to the Holy Spirit's direction.

So I continued writing, and in addition to the Lord providing to me inspiration for the book gleaned from my own personal experiences and the Scriptures, He began orchestrating opportunities for me to meet many people who had remarkable stories to tell about their own experiences with the miraculous. And I retell some of their stories in this book.

God has led many people into my path (or me into theirs) so they could share their experiences with me. Again and again after listening to their testimonies of God's graciousness and power, I have walked away in amazement of all God has done in the lives of His children. What He did in the life of Chase Lynch of Gulf Shores, Alabama is no exception.

His story is just another example of how our God knows no limits.

In May of 2018 I was scheduled to speak at a women's conference in Alabama. My family and I decided to extend the trip and drive down to Gulf Shores for some rest and relaxation on the beach. We booked lodging, but unfortunately, subtropical storm Alberto also had plans to go to the beach that weekend.

It was too late to get a refund of our lodging payment, so we ended up rescheduling the family trip for September.

September actually turned out to be the best time to go, though. Things had slowed down drastically. The beaches were practically bare compared to the middle of summer, and traffic was light. We checked into the condo we had rented and rested up for the next day. The following day was my birthday, and after a great morning at the beach and some shopping, my husband took me to my favorite restaurant.

After leaving the restaurant, on the way back to the condo we noticed the cutest little Airstream trailer and a sign that displayed the words "Frost Bites Shave Ice." This family loves shaved ice, so there was no question about stopping.

As we approached the trailer and placed our orders, the man at the window—whom I would soon come to know as Chase— asked where we were from. As the small talk continued we got on the topic of music. Knowing we were from Tennessee, Chase asked me if I liked Country music. I told him I didn't listen to anything but Christian music. His eyes lit up as he exclaimed, "Me too!"

Chase's mother, Elisa, was whipping up my shaved ice. And when she finished, she joined our conversation about God and faith.

Elisa then began to share with me that Chase was her *miracle* baby, and she told me how God had miraculously spared his life multiple times. As she began to share his story with me I knew our encounter was planned in advance by our heavenly Father.

Chase was born in May of 1984 in a difficult delivery. After seventeen long hours of labor, the doctors decided to use forceps to aid the delivery process. Unfortunately, too much pressure was applied with the forceps, and within a few hours after delivery baby Chase began to have light seizures. He was then sent by ambulance to a larger hospital with a neonatal unit in Lake Charles, Louisiana.

There the doctors determined that Chase had a subdural hematoma, which meant there was bleeding between his brain and skull, and he would need an operation to stop the bleeding. Of course that was devastating news to Elisa and her husband, Pat, and they began calling friends all over the country to begin to pray.

By that time Chase was being kept alive only by life support systems. And while on life support his little body started retaining fluids and became so swollen that a person could scarcely make out his facial features.

Before long, after deciding it would be better for Chase to be treated by an experienced neurosurgeon, the medical team in Lake Charles arranged to have Chase airlifted to Ochsner Medical

Center in New Orleans that same night. Unable to fly with Chase, Pat and Elisa made the drive to New Orleans in their car.

After they joined Chase at the hospital, Elisa and her husband were informed that their baby would have surgery at seven o'clock the following morning. Pat and Elisa tried to mentally prepare themselves for their baby's surgery as they left the hospital that night.

Early the next morning they returned to the hospital, and that's when they experienced the first of several miracles in Chase's life.

When they walked into Chase's hospital room they saw that Chase was off all life support systems. The fluid was gone, and he was sucking on a pacifier. They were amazed to see their baby boy with just a bump on his head, and that completely disappeared over time.

Chase's doctors prescribed anti-seizure medication for him and informed his parents that in the future he might have trouble with coordination. But to God's glory, Chase was off all medication by the age of four and was able to play sports and enjoy all the activities he loved.

But before he turned five, he and his parents faced another daunting experience. One morning when Chase woke up, he had a fever and complained of not feeling well. By midday Chase was lethargic. His parents were concerned about his declining condition and took him to the doctor. His doctor immediately called an airlift team and arranged to have him transported once again to Ochsner's in New Orleans.

Chase was diagnosed at the hospital with Spinal Meningitis. Once again Elisa and Pat enlisted prayer warriors to join them in praying for little Chase, and once again God heard their prayers. Chase spent two weeks in Ochsner Medical Center and miraculously—by the grace and power of God—walked away with no apparent side effects.

All seemed to be well after that as Chase continued to grow into a healthy young adult. But in 2010 yet another life-threatening health problem struck his life. Chase had a bad seizure and was seen by a neurologist who put him back on seizure medication as they continued to test him to search for the cause of the seizure.

An MRI[26] was ordered, and after the test results arrived the neurologist regretfully informed Chase and his parents that he had a brain tumor.

The doctor referred Chase to a neurosurgeon, and the neurosurgeon discovered the tumor was located in an extremely fragile location in his brain. He prepared Chase and his parents for the worst and explained the extreme danger of damage that could be caused by simply going in to take a biopsy of the tumor.

Though filled with apprehension, the family agreed that they had no choice but to go forward with the surgery. Chase was scheduled for surgery, and prayers again ascended into heaven for yet another miracle.

When Chase arrived at the hospital for the operation, the surgery team conducted a final MRI for the neurosurgeon to use for reference during the surgery. But astonishingly, the results of the MRI showed no tumor in Chase's brain. It was gone!

According to what Elisa told me, she wept in relief after they received the news. Then the doctor shared with them that his

---

26 Magnetic Resonance Imaging (MRI)—a medical imaging procedure used to generate images of the organs in the body.

father was a minister, and he was a believer as well. He also told them that he believed in the power of prayer, and in Chase's case there was no other explanation for the disappearance of the tumor.

Chase continued for the next two years on his seizure medication and was frequently seen by a neurologist who ordered occasional tests to make sure the tumor hadn't reappeared. Chase had no seizures, and no changes in the tests showed up during that two-year period.

But in 2012 Chase began having seizures again, and they often caused him to fall to the ground. His doctor increased the seizure medication, but Chase wasn't responding to the medication, and the seizures continued.

Then once again Chase and his family were faced with a terrible reality. An MRI revealed another brain tumor. Elisa was angry at first and didn't understand how it could be possible. She told me she wondered if the doctors missed the tumor in earlier tests. But regardless, once again they were facing devastating news.

To make matters worse for Chase and his family, Chase had just graduated from broadcasting school and had no insurance. The family not only had to find a neurosurgeon but also had to figure out how to pay for the surgery.

When they finally found a neurosurgeon who was available for the surgery, he informed them after examining Chase that the tumor was in a location where surgery would do more harm than good. He suggested that Chase just try to live out the remainder of his life the best he could.

Unwilling to accept the neurosurgeon's prognosis, though, the family went to their pastor for prayer and guidance. Their pastor suggested they try getting Chase into MD Anderson for treatment.[27]

Chase and his parents renewed their search for a surgeon who would treat Chase's tumor. Because of the tumor's location, and because the type of tumor Chase had was so rare, it turned out that after a tiring search there were only three doctors in the world who would touch Chase's tumor.

And one of those doctors practiced at MD Anderson.

MD Anderson not only had the right doctor, but the staff there also helped Elisa find assistance to cover all of Chase's expenses.

Elisa told me she knew God was at work once again. And as Elisa and Chase continued to relate the events to me as I stood that evening listening to them at their shaved ice stand, I was filled with anticipation to hear yet another instance of God demonstrating His unlimited ability to overcome what seemed like an impossibility.

Chase was soon scheduled for surgery, and the surgery was no small task. Chase's surgery took more than ten hours to complete. The surgery was not only difficult, it turned out to be complicated by some leftover effects of the spinal meningitis that Chase suffered when he was a child.

After the surgery the surgeon informed Chase's parents that he was disappointed that he was able to remove only sixty-five percent of the tumor. But Elisa was encouraged when she later

---

27 MD Anderson is a hospital with a main campus in Houston, Texas. It is associated with The University of Texas and maintains a well-known cancer treatment and research center.

found out that the surgeon was a Christian and prayed over his patients before surgery. The surgeon told her that he believed God played His part in helping him throughout the surgery.

While Chase was still in the hospital recovering, he had what is called a *mini stroke*. As a result, Chase lost his ability to swallow, and the hospital staff began therapy to help with that. A week of therapy passed, and still he was unable to eat. Elisa met with the doctor, and he told her Chase would likely go home to live the rest of his life depending on a feeding tube.

Elisa was of course upset and walked out of the room to let her husband know what the doctor said.

Through bitter tears they both began to pray. Once Elisa had finished praying and regained her composure, she walked back into Chase's room and found him in the bathroom brushing his teeth. And he could swallow! Chase and his parents experienced yet another miracle.

Before Chase was discharged from the hospital to go home, his doctor told him and his parents that he felt it could be ten years or more before they would see any growth of his tumor, if at all, so they left Houston feeling good about Chase's prognosis.

Chase went through twelve months of chemotherapy after going home from the hospital. And over the next three years he received an MRI every three months to monitor what was left of the tumor.

Chase lived a normal life over that three-year period with no further complications in his health. However, an MRI at the end of that period showed his tumor had changed. Chase and his parents were faced with another decision.

The physicians at MD Anderson wanted to use Proton Radiation to destroy the tumor. However, it was extremely expensive and hard to get approved for payment by insurance. But once again the people at MD Anderson worked with the insurance company and were able to get it approved.

After approval, Chase spent six weeks in Houston going to the hospital every day for treatment. The Proton Radiation was able to get rid of another fifteen percent of the tumor compared to its original size, so by the end of those treatments a full eighty percent of the tumor was gone.

Chase's seizure medication has been reduced since then, and at this writing he has had good reports for the last three years. It has now been six years since his operation, and Chase is living a full and productive life.

Elisa said to me, "Chase is a miracle, and we know that God has saved him so he can tell his story."

Then she said, "Chase's favorite saying is 'Never give up.'"

Sometimes we are indeed tempted to give up when we're severely challenged. Our battles may tire us, and it may feel like the things we experience are wearing us down. But Elisa and Chase would have no problem telling anyone that there are miracles birthed in the hope that remains ours in even our weakest moments.

King David, the great Psalmist, wrote:

Guide me by your truth and teach me, for you are God my Savior, and my hope is in you all day long. (Psalm 25:5)

David knew well God's abilities to lead him and teach him the things he needed to learn. And he also knew how God delivered him and saved him from his enemies. David experienced those things, and he learned through his experiences to pray and place his hope confidently in God through every challenge no matter the severity.

There was no bear, or lion, or giant, or anything else that could overtake and destroy David as long as God was with him. He learned to put an unwavering hope in God. He learned to trust God even in his deepest times of discouragement.

Like David, Chase learned by experience that he can trust God too. And as Chase gives others his personal testimony of the miraculous healings he experienced, he is certainly qualified to say with confidence and authority, "Never give up."

That is always good advice for anyone. But especially for those of us who put our faith and trust in God, it should be gladly embraced. Our God clearly lives and operates outside of the limitations we experience in life. He is unlimited in His abilities. And He alone is the author of our salvation, always our help in time of trouble,[28] and the one, true *God of Healing and Miracles.*

I was incredibly blessed that day when Elisa shared Chase's story with me. I left Frost Bites Shave Ice that afternoon enjoying the special treats I had received. The shaved ice was delicious, but the spiritual nourishment I received by meeting Chase and Elisa meant so much more to me.

---

28 "God is our refuge and strength, an ever-present help in trouble. Therefore we will not fear, though the earth give way and the mountains fall into the heart of the sea, though its waters roar and foam and the mountains quake with their surging" (Psalm 46:1-3).

Our Lord is extremely creative. He often performs miracles in ways that cannot be attributed to anyone's assistance or to any force on earth. But He also can demonstrate His miraculous nature and work through people by equipping and using them to bring to others the miracles they need.

God uses His followers in miraculous ways. He always has. And He used believing doctors and other medical staff to assist in some of the miracles He was bringing to Chase. But He also brought healing to Chase in ways that rise above all human understanding and knowledge.

Remember this: "God uses things in His work, but He also still makes things out of nothing."[29]

I for one don't care how God chooses to deliver the miracles we need. I simply long to see Him do it—because miracles testify of God's truth, bring glory to Him, and usher in life to those who receive them.

We need to believe God for miracles. We need to pray for others to receive the miracles they need. And when we ourselves are challenged by sobering or frightening realities—when we ourselves need nothing short of a miracle to survive—we need to pray and trust God for that miracle.

We need to press on and ask fellow believers to pray with us, too. We need to let them know we're not giving up. We're going to God for help.

Miracles happen every day, and they're all around us. In our rush through life we just don't always take the time to recognize them. And sometimes, perhaps, we just drive by them without

---

29 I quote words spoken recently by L. Edward Hazelbaker, used by permission.

knowing they are there. I'm glad I didn't do that. There are miracles to meet. And there are miracles to experience!

Don't limit what God can do in your life and the lives of those you love.

Believe, have faith, and never give up!

CHAPTER 8

Trembling Darkness

AS YOU BEGIN reading this chapter I need you to know right up front that it contains content about demon possession and the casting out of demons. If you want to avoid reading about or dealing with this subject you are free to move on. But demon possession exists, and we should both understand it and address it.

The activity of evil spirits is real, and it is something that is not relegated to the past in the stories of Scripture. Neither is it something that exists only in some deep, dark jungle somewhere seen only by foreign missionaries.

Demon possession exists today. It exists even in the most developed countries—including America. Evil spirits are active in the communities where we live. And dealing with them is still part of spiritual warfare.

I initially hesitated to include the topic of demon possession in this book because I am well aware of how people can react to talking about such things. Some people are critical of anyone who speaks frankly and honestly about dealing with demon possession. And I admit that I, myself, have sometimes been skeptical when I've heard others speak about this topic.

In fact, quite honestly, when I've heard some people talk about dealing with demon-possessed people, I thought they might have overactive imaginations or just be . . . well . . . a little flaky if you know what I mean.

Having been born to Bible-believing Christian parents and raised in church, though, I have heard all my life about demon possession. And I've read in the Bible every instance of Jesus and the disciples casting out unclean spirits and releasing from darkness those who were bound by demons.

I have always known dealing with demons was biblical, and I accepted that it was definitely possible even today, so I can't really explain why I found it so difficult to believe people who shared their experiences about it happening in this day and age.

But that has all changed!

I have a dear friend who also works in jail ministry. Some time ago she was telling me a story about one of her experiences when she had to cast a demon out of a lady in a jail service. I have a lot of respect for her, and I know she is not one to exaggerate the truth. I'm sure my eyes grew wide with amazement as she told me exactly what happened.

After she told me her story, she looked at me and said, "Donna, you will surely experience this at some point yourself in ministering in jails. These incarcerated ladies have abused drugs and altered their minds so many times. Others have dabbled in the occult and witchcraft. It seems they have opened themselves up wide to demonic spirits without even realizing it."

I couldn't help but think, "Oh, I hope I don't have to experience this—ever."

Fast forward about a year:

A lady I had ministered to in the jail (and who had been released) called me and asked if I could come to her house because she was certain she had been possessed by a demon. I asked her what made her think that had happened, and she told me she was hearing voices and doing things that she normally wouldn't do.

She begged me to come to her house and cast out the demon.

I must admit my curiosity was peaked. "Is this going to be the encounter my friend told me I was sure to face?" I wondered.

I told the lady I would stop by after I finished ministering at the jail that morning. When I arrived I could tell she was high on something, and she began to tell me there were snakes in the air-conditioning vents talking to her.

I looked her in the eye and asked, "When was the last time you used?"

She informed me that she had used meth two days earlier.

I said, "The only demon in this house is you!" I was so exasperated!

She had been clean for well over a year, but in the past few months she had relapsed and seemed to be doing things that were worse than she had ever done in the past. Honestly, I was a little angry with her, but mostly I was angry with the enemy.

He just never gives up!

I talked to her, prayed for her, and explained that she didn't have a demon at that point. But I told her if she continued on that path she could certainly attract one.

A few weeks later I was getting ready to go to the jail and have church with the ladies. As I drove to the jail I was listening to worship music playing on the radio. I was simply focusing on the goodness of God when the presence of the Holy Spirit just flooded the car. And I began to pray in tongues.

I couldn't hold back the river that was flowing from deep within me. I was so blessed at that time to feel the Lord's presence in such a wonderful way.

I arrived at the jail, and once inside, twelve ladies joined me for the service. I prayed, and we began to sing worship songs. As we continued to worship I noticed an older lady with her arms raised. She had never been in the service before. I'm always blessed to see the ladies with their arms raised and tears streaming down their faces in worship to God.

But that lady seemed a little *different*, and I felt I should continue to watch her.

As the music continued to play, and as the other ladies continued to sing, I made my way toward the one who seemed to be acting odd. When I approached her she turned to face the wall and mouthed something I could not understand. I placed my hand on her shoulder to pray for her, and it was as if the Holy Spirit spoke to me and said, "That is not my Spirit."

She immediately fell to the floor and started trying to bang her head on the concrete.

Realizing what I was facing, I whispered, "Help me, Holy Spirit."

I then turned to the eleven other ladies and explained to them what was going on. I asked them to check their hearts and ask Jesus to forgive them of any sin in their lives and ask Him to be their Lord.

I explained, "This lady has a demon, and when I cast it out, it will look for the next available vessel. Don't be that vessel. Make things right with God right now!"

By that time the lady was starting to foam at the mouth. Her arms were curved in toward her body, and her right leg was somehow bent up behind her. Her arms and legs were stiff as if she couldn't unfold them. I tried to get her to look at me but she wouldn't. I was holding her head to keep her from banging it into the wall and floor.

I was thinking, "I should have read more information about what to do in this situation. I've never cast out a demon before. God, please help me."

She still wouldn't look at me, and it was as if the Holy Spirit gently whispered to me, "Make her look at you."

She was not at all responsive to me as I asked her to look at my face, so I physically turned her head toward me. Her eyes glazed over right before my eyes with what appeared to be thick cataracts.

The whole time I was thinking, "Is this really happening?"

Still, I was amazed by the total absence of fear or doubt in me. I knew the Holy Spirit was empowering me and leading me through that situation. Otherwise, I am certain I would not have had the boldness or faith to do what I did next.

I turned around and noticed that three corrections officers had come into the room with us. All three stood back and did not come near us. That in itself was extremely unusual because the officers are required to remove inmates who get on the floor for any reason or appear to be disrupting the service.

In the next moment I looked straight into the lady's eyes and said, "You have to come out of her in the name of Jesus!"

She continued to try to mouth something, but it was as if her jaw was totally locked, and she continued to foam at the mouth. She still avoided looking at me. Once again holding her head in my hands to prevent her from hurting herself, I again turned her face toward me and commanded the unclean spirit to come out in the name of Jesus.

She was still writhing and foaming at the mouth, so once more I said, "You have no power or authority here, and you *must* come out now in the name of Jesus!"

She then looked at me, and her eyes became clear. She sat up, and I asked her if she was okay. She said she was fine. I asked her if she was ready to accept Christ as her Savior. She gave me a resounding yes, and I immediately prayed with her and led her to Christ.

She told me and the other ladies at the table that was the first time in years that she felt like she was in control of her own body. The other ladies began to comment that she looked so different and that even her voice sounded different. She thanked me, and she thanked me over and over again.

I told her to thank *Jesus*, because *He* rescued her—He did it!

The corrections officers left the room, and I continued the service using the opportunity to point out the importance of surrendering our lives to Christ and staying sober. I explained to the ladies that when we alter our mind with drugs, alcohol, or other destructive influences, we open ourselves up to demon possession or oppression.

When the ladies left the room to return to their cell blocks, one of the jailers told me to wait at the desk because the head corrections officer wanted to talk to me. I was thinking, "Oh boy. This is it. They are never going to let me come back."

The head corrections officer soon approached me and said, "I just want to ask you *one* question. Are you sure you got them all?"

I assured her that they were gone.

She and the other corrections officer at the desk continued to tell me that the ladies had been having nightmares and seeing strange dark shadows when no one was there. She told me they all just felt an evil presence and informed me that it all started when that particular lady came into the jail.

The head corrections officer then said, "I knew what was going on, so I didn't want to interrupt. I am so glad you were here and knew exactly what to do."

I then assured her it was the Holy Spirit who led me through the whole thing.

As I left the jail that day, I reflected on my drive to the jail earlier that morning, and I remembered how the Holy Spirit had flooded my car with His presence.

I then knew beyond a shadow of a doubt that He was preparing me for what I was about to face. I didn't know it at the time, but the Lord was going to use me that day to demonstrate His power to bring deliverance to someone extremely bound.

God used that experience to drive home to me that we—you and I who serve Him—must be prepared to release prisoners from darkness. And I'm not just talking about people who are prisoners inside a jail. I'm talking about anyone who is bound by the powers of darkness.

Here is what the prophet Isaiah wrote over 2,700 years ago as he spoke of the coming of Jesus in his Messianic prophecy recorded in Isaiah chapter sixty-one:

> *The Spirit of the Sovereign Lord is on me, because the Lord has anointed me to proclaim good news to the poor. He has sent me to bind up the brokenhearted, to proclaim freedom for the captives and release from darkness for the prisoners.*
>
> (Isaiah 61:1)

During His years of ministry on earth, Jesus went about doing the exact things Isaiah said He would do, and that included delivering the demon possessed from the darkness of their imprisonment.

But Jesus went beyond just doing that himself. He also sent His disciples out—even before His resurrection and ascension to heaven—to take His message to those in need of spiritual help. And that included delivering the demon possessed.

We read in the tenth chapter of the Gospel of Luke of the time Jesus sent out seventy-two of His followers, two by two, to go ahead of Him into many towns before He arrived. In the seventeenth verse we read that when His followers returned from their ministry in the towns they were rejoicing in what they were able to accomplish.

And they said, *"Lord, even the demons submit to us in your name"* (v.17).

By that, we know that His followers were not only proclaiming the good news and binding up the brokenhearted, they were also proclaiming *freedom for the captives* and releasing prisoners from darkness. That is, they were also delivering spiritual captives from demon possession just as the Lord was doing.

But in case anyone wants to doubt God's intention for His followers to do this level of ministry, there is more in the Gospels about it. Matthew wrote that Jesus also called the twelve disciples together and likewise sent them out to do His work of ministry.

Jesus called his twelve disciples to him and gave them authority to drive out impure spirits and to heal every disease and sickness.

These twelve Jesus sent out with the following instructions: "... As you go, proclaim this message: 'The kingdom of heaven has come near.' Heal the sick, raise the dead, cleanse those who have leprosy, drive out demons. Freely you have received; freely give." (Matthew 10:1, 5-8)

And Mark wrote the following in his gospel account about the work Jesus appointed the disciples to do:

Then Jesus went around teaching from village to village. Calling the Twelve to him, he began to send them out two by two and gave them authority over impure spirits.

They went out and preached that people should repent. They drove out many demons and anointed many sick people with oil and healed them. (Mark 6:6b-7, 12-13)

Many people—even many well-meaning Christians—would like to ignore the seriousness of the spiritual battles going on around us. But we ignore the reality of warring against demonic powers and influences at our own peril—and at a cost of not meeting the needs of those to whom we are to carry the Gospel.

Within the Great Commission given to the followers of Christ is God's desire for us to not only carry the good news to the world but to also be involved in doing the things that God is still doing in the world through the Holy Spirit.

The work of God is the work of the Church, and none of that work should be categorized as no longer important. Anticipating the Great Commission, and projecting the work of the Church that Jesus was establishing to carry out His mission on earth, Jesus spoke these words to His disciples:[30]

Very truly I tell you, whoever believes in me will do the works I have been doing, and they will do even greater things than these, because I am going to the Father. (John 14:12)

Clearly, we are to do the same work on earth now that Jesus did on earth during His ministry. And beyond any doubt, His mission is still being carried out by the Holy Spirit.

We must be involved in doing battle with the enemy of our souls, and we should not hesitate to come against evil. We must have the spiritual discernment to recognize what is happening around us, and we must be ready to act.

---

30 I recognize that I quote John 14:12 more than once in this book. But that is because what Jesus said to His disciples before completing His earthly work and returning to heaven has huge implications on His intention for us and our ministries. These words need to sink deeply into all our hearts and not only inspire us but also cause us to feel the heartbeat of God.

The lady I met in the prison that day had been bound for years by that demon. She later told me of the horrible things it had spoken to her over the years, and she told me that it had once physically thrown her out of a moving car.

That certainly sounds shocking, but it shouldn't really surprise us. After all, the devil and his minions are all about destroying God's kingdom and the hope that anyone will ever come to know and trust Jesus.

But remember, we have a Father in heaven who is far more powerful than any spirit of darkness! As I continued my drive home from the jail that day, one of my favorite worship songs came on the radio. One line of the lyrics is:

"Jesus, Jesus, you make the darkness tremble."[31]

That morning in the jail, I personally witnessed the darkness tremble. But it wasn't until I heard that song's lyrics that the reality of what I had just experienced came to me with force. I had just witnessed the power of darkness having to flee in the *Name of Jesus.*

I then thought of those disciples as they ran to Jesus and told Him that even the demons were subject to them. I chuckled to myself because I had felt that same amazement, and I could certainly relate to their excitement. Then I remembered Jesus' response:

He replied, "I saw Satan fall like lightning from heaven. I have given you authority to trample on snakes and scorpions and to overcome all the power of the enemy; nothing will harm

---

31 From the song *Tremble*, recorded by Mosaic MSC, https://www. essentialworship.com/songs/mosaic-msc/tremble

you. However, do not rejoice that the spirits submit to you, but rejoice that your names are written in heaven."

(Luke 10:18-20)

With our names recorded in the Lamb's book of life, we can have confidence in God and know that He is not surprised by anything that comes our way. We can come to understand that we can trust Him to lead and orchestrate our lives and ministries for His glory.

And as we come to understand that our relationship with God is the greatest miracle of all, we will be able to put all the other miraculous things God does in our lives and through our ministries in the proper perspective.

The way I look at it, we are the children of the *Most High God*. And when we are involved in bringing God's authority and power to bear against any power or obstacle, He is simply sharing with His children His authority and power. Christians should not be amazed with such things—even though we sometimes are.

Our Lord is Lord of all. He is all-powerful, and nothing is impossible for Him. Through the continuing work of the Holy Spirit—and through the Church—Jesus is still proclaiming freedom and releasing prisoners from darkness.

And before Him, the darkness definitely trembles.

CHAPTER 9

Desiring Answers

SOMETIMES WE CAN feel limited when it seems God isn't answering our prayers. I can't tell you how many times after praying that I have wondered if God was even listening to me, because I felt He was slow to answer. Perhaps you can think of times when you felt the same way.

When we are attempting to do God's work and desire answers from God, and they don't seem to come, we can feel like limitations are being placed on us. When answers seem slow to come, it can even make us feel like we lack God's favor.

We may feel like an unanswered prayer is a sign indicating God is disappointed in us. But that can be far from the truth. Sometimes the prayer has already been answered. Sometimes we just haven't recognized the answer. And sometimes that's because the answer was provided to us in the *silence* of our heavenly Father.

There was a particular time when I prayed for a certain position in women's leadership. I relentlessly begged God to place me in the position, but I heard nothing back from Him. The absence of His voice was overwhelming.

I felt like God had gone completely silent. But I continued to give the Lord all the reasons why I believed that particular position would be perfect for me. I was almost certain He would answer, and the position would be mine.

Oh, how the position would open so many doors for me and my ministry! I knew it would, and everything about it had my name on it. I thought that was what God wanted, so I could do more for Him. I believed it surely must be God's plan to put me into that highly-coveted position. Still, I received no answer.

Eventually, though, the answer became fully evident, and to my chagrin it was not the answer I had hoped for. Someone else was selected for the position.

I was happy for her. Life went on, and a couple of weeks later I had all but forgotten about the position that I was so certain had been custom designed for me.

Then a few months later I was asked to join a group of women in another, yet lower position of leadership. I prayed about it and accepted the opportunity. I didn't realize at the time what God was up to, but I soon caught on. God was altering my view. From my previously limited viewpoint I *thought* the position I prayed for would be perfect for me.

But God knew better.

After begging God and pleading for something I *wanted*, I was moved into a position that allowed me to see firsthand what I would have had to endure if the position actually had been given to me. I can't tell you how many times since then that I have thanked God for not answering that prayer the way I wanted Him to answer it.

I have since reflected several times on how what I once assumed was negligence on God's part in not answering my prayer turned out completely the opposite. He wasn't negligent; He was absolutely blessing me.

Knowing what I know now, I can honestly say I would never desire that position for me. In no shape, form, or fashion was it ever designed for me. I now diligently pray for and encourage the woman God moved into the position I once desired, and I am so glad He appointed someone who *could* handle all the demands of that job.

God knows us very well, and He always has our best interests in mind when He makes decisions that affect our futures.

Of course there are times when God's silence is not the issue when it comes to feeling like we are failing to receive answers to our prayers. Sometimes God answers us in a clear way—and sometimes with no delay—but we choose to have selective hearing. And because of that, we fail to accept the answer that has already been delivered.

We can be guilty of becoming aware of God's answer but tuning it out because it's not the answer we want. In hindsight I can think of a few times when I asked God for something, and I heard but ignored God's voice whispering to my heart, "This is not my plan for you."

I quickly dismissed that answer and attempted to convince myself that it was just my imagination.

But deep down I had a certain gnawing, knowing feeling that I had heard God's voice. It was a feeling that just wouldn't go away. I had a deep sense of knowing that I wasn't going to get what I was praying for—or at least not exactly in the way I expected it—but I refused to accept it.

We must always be careful to listen to God even if we're not hearing the answers we are hoping for. And we may as well accept all His answers, because ignoring the ones we don't want to hear won't change them.

It is always best to not only listen for but respond in humility and faith to the answers God provides. In doing so we will always find that our Good Father is wisely and lovingly directing our lives.

We can perceive God isn't answering our prayers because we don't see God's answer in His silence. And we can be guilty of not receiving God's answer because we don't really want to hear it. But there is another reason why we can have problems receiving answers from the Lord. Here is what James has to say about that:

> *You do not have because you don't ask God. When you ask, you do not receive, because you ask with wrong motives, that you may spend what you get on your pleasures.* (James 4:2b-3)

James dealt with several things in his short book in the New Testament. Among those is prayer and receiving answers from God. James first made it clear that God's people must ask God for the things they need. That is of course done in prayer.

James encouraged his readers to go to God with their

requests. But then he told them their requests could be denied if they prayed with the wrong motives.

If we are being completely honest, many of us (if not most or all of us) have prayed prayers with a wrong motive at one time or another. Our flesh gives us problems, and we need help with this. But even Christian leaders who counsel us in the ways of the Lord can deal unsuccessfully with temptations when it comes to motives.

So to look for the best illustration of what can be accomplished by a person who always prays with the right motives, let's look to Jesus.

While the Bible contains many records of Jesus ministering to and praying for others, there are few accounts of how Jesus prayed for himself. But we know He separated himself from His followers from time to time so He could be alone to pray. And there was one time when He separated himself from His disciples that stands out more than all others.

It's in that particular time of prayer that we see clearly into the motivation that affected how Jesus prayed for himself.

Then Jesus went with his disciples to a place called Gethsemane, and he said to them, "Sit here while I go over there and pray." He took Peter and the two sons of Zebedee along with him, and he began to be sorrowful and troubled. Then he said to them, "My soul is overwhelmed with sorrow to the point of death. Stay here and keep watch with me."

Going a little farther, he fell with his face to the ground and prayed, "My Father, if it is possible, may this cup be taken from me. Yet not as I will, but as you will." (Matthew 26:36-39)

There is no better window into the motives that drove Jesus when presenting His own needs to the Father than the prayer He prayed prior to giving His life for us as a sacrifice for sins, so we can be saved. He actually prayed to be relieved of the terrifying responsibility that had been placed upon Him.

That prayer appears to have been answered with silence. But Jesus also prayed for His Father's will to be done, and the Father revealed to Jesus His answer to that prayer that very night. Jesus accepted the answer, and God's will was accomplished both in and through Him the next day.

Jesus' prayers were not motivated by fame, fortune, or anything else the world had to offer Him. His prayers were not motivated by either desired notoriety or position. While Christ's motives were questioned by others—by His enemies and accusers—His motivation in seeking answers from God for His own needs was unquestionably right and noble.

And when it came to ministering to and praying for others—when it came to seeking answers and solutions for them—Christ's motivation could likewise not have been more honorable.

Jesus went through all the towns and villages, teaching in their synagogues, proclaiming the good news of the kingdom and healing every disease and sickness. When he saw the crowds, he had compassion on them, because they were harassed and helpless like sheep without a shepherd. (Matthew 9:35-36)

Jesus had great compassion on the people, and that's what motivated Jesus to pray for and minister to the people around Him. Is that our motivation? When we pray for people, do we look beyond their disease and sickness and think about their spiritual condition?

That's what Jesus did!

If our motivation for praying for miracles of healing and deliverance go beyond what we see in people's physical conditions, we will be more like Jesus. And if our concern is more focused on sharing Christ's love and concern for souls, our prayers for miracles will be more effective.

In a world that is being so overcome with selfishness and hatred, people need to know that some of us still have true, godly compassion for others. They need to see Jesus in us. I believe when we get to the place where our hearts break for the wandering, the lost, and the broken, we will experience the kind of compassion Jesus had for people.

And God will honor our prayers.

When we are truly moved with the kind of compassion Jesus had for the people surrounding Him, our motives will line up with His motives, and our prayers will be answered. If our motives are right, we will desperately want to see people healed and delivered—but above all, saved. And our focus in all of that will be on wanting God to receive all the glory for what is accomplished.

We won't succumb to a temptation to accept for ourselves any of the glory attributed to our answered prayers, because we know it all belongs to Jesus. And we won't be concerned about building reputations as faith healers or miracle workers.

When we take the message of Christ to others and pray for people to be healed, to be delivered, or to receive any other miracle they need from God, we will be motivated to do so only because of our concern for *them* and our desire to please God.

When it comes to praying, if our motives align with those of our Lord's, we can expect to receive wonderful answers from God!

But what happens when we pray for someone for years, and still the miracle we're praying for doesn't come? That can be challenging.

My mom was injured in a four-wheeler accident years ago. Because of the accident she was paralyzed from the chest down. As of this writing she has been in a wheelchair for eighteen years. I can't tell you how many times I have prayed for her healing. Actually, I've never stopped praying for her healing.

Who could you love and have more compassion for than your own mother? I know my compassion for her is complete, and I certainly trust that my motives for asking for her healing are right. But even though there have been times when I have felt absolutely certain that God was going to heal her—I just knew we were going to witness a miracle—her condition has not changed.

I was invited to speak for a women's event at a nearby church one particular night. My mom was planning to attend as well as some friends and other members of my family. Before I went there to speak, God poured into my heart a very powerful message about healing.

I looked at all the circumstances surrounding that service, and I just knew without a doubt, that night was going to be the night my mom got out of her wheelchair. It seemed like I had goosebumps for days before I even got to the church to speak. I truly felt like God had asked me to step out in faith for what appeared impossible.

As I spent time praying and worshipping God several times before the service, I burst into tears, and my heart overflowed with joy and thankfulness for what God was about to do.

I was so *sure* my mom was going to be healed that my own excitement overflowed and inspired my teenage daughters as well. They also believed wholeheartedly that their grandmother was going to walk that night.

I arrived at the church, and it seemed as if the very air was charged with electricity. As I preached, the Holy Spirit just began to pour into me everything He had purposed for me to say. I had never felt so powerfully inspired. When I preached, the message seemed to flow out of me like a river. I was literally trembling the whole time I was speaking.

When I gave the altar call, I asked my mom to come forward.

I asked for the women in the church to come and surround her so we could pray for her. I took a giant leap of faith, and I began to pray with an expectancy like I had never felt before. I even tried to pull her up onto her feet. But nothing happened. I prayed again, and again, and again as I repeated the process.

Still nothing happened!

You better believe I definitely desired some answers after I left the church that night. I felt like God had let me down. I was upset, embarrassed, heartbroken for my mom and daughters, and determined to never step out and pray for anyone's healing ever again.

I was so discouraged.

A few days later I received a phone call from a pastor somewhere in Pennsylvania. I'm still not sure how he learned about me. He asked me several questions about my ministry. Then he asked me if I had a healing ministry.

I thought, "That's an odd question to ask completely out of the blue."

Before I even realized what was going on, though, I was pouring my heart out to the pastor about the service in which I prayed for my mom and how I had been so sure that she was going to receive her healing before I even arrived at the church.

I told him of all my intense fellowship with God when I literally wept before the Lord and poured out my praise in thanksgiving for what He was going to do. I told him I had never felt so sure of anything in my life, and I just knew my mom was going to be healed.

Then I told him about how my mother didn't receive her healing and how I had felt so let down. I told him that I didn't feel like I could even preach on healing or miracles again.

I'll never forget the next thing that pastor said to me.

He said, "God *has* called you into a healing ministry. You *will* speak on healing and miracles again, and you *will* see healing and miracles. God knows you have faith for miracles, but now He wants to see if you truly believe in who He is *without* the expected outcome."

He continued, "I know it would have been an overwhelming testimony to share that God had miraculously healed your mom— and He may yet. But the greater testimony is that you continue to preach on healing and miracles. The greater testimony comes from you telling people that God may not have done it in that particular instance, but that you still believe He is the same yesterday, today, and forever.[32]

"Real faith," he said, "is demonstrated by continuing to pray for the hundredth person just as fervently as you prayed for the first one even if none of the previous ninety-nine were healed. When God is ready to answer, He will. In the meantime, you have to trust Him as the Sovereign God He is and continue to preach like you did before He *didn't* answer your prayer for the miracle."

To this day, I still wonder who that pastor was. I can't remember his name, but I know our conversation was a divine appointment. I know the *God of Miracles*, and I received a powerful, miraculous answer from God that day.

The prophet Habakkuk experienced sorrowful trouble and had to face challenges to his faith in God. He had critical questions about what God was allowing to happen to the nation of Judah. God was executing judgment upon the nation by allowing their enemies to overcome them, and Habakkuk complained in prayer that it was not fair to allow a nation more corrupt than they were to judge them.

God was of course more than both fair and righteous in His actions—while Habakkuk was wrong in his thinking. Habakkuk didn't like God's answer to his appeals, but he came to accept God's sovereignty. In the end Habakkuk made a powerful declaration of his faith and determination to continue to follow and trust God.

---

32 Hebrews 13:8.

Though the fig tree does not bud
and there are no grapes on the vines,
though the olive crop fails
and the fields produce no food,
though there are no sheep in the pen
and no cattle in the stalls,
yet I will rejoice in the Lord,
I will be joyful in God my Savior.   (Habakkuk 3:17-18)

Habakkuk came to accept that God had both a reason and a right to do what He was doing. Initially He didn't like the way God answered him when he called out in prayer, but in the end he not only retained his faith in God and accepted the Lord's will but also determined to rejoice in Him through every circumstance.

God's actions are always righteous. He does not randomly limit us on a whim by choosing which prayers to answer or which prayers to ignore. He simply knows best, and He is working in the middle of all things—through all our circumstances—for our good.[33] We must therefore, at all times, practice patience in all we do and surrender our will to God.

We desire answers when we pray and communicate with our Savior, and God wants us to continue that with all our hearts. And regardless of how or when God answers, this is what I know to be true:

There is no limit to God's ability to heal, save, deliver, and perform miracles. And it's a good thing to desire answers from

---

33 "And we know that in all things God works for the good of those who love him, who have been called according to his purpose" (Romans 8:28).

God. We need to maintain that desire until the time comes when we will know *all* the answers.

I have decided that even if I disappoint the Lord (and myself) in the future through my inability to receive His answers the way I should, I will continue to pray for myself and others, and anticipate answers from God. And I will also continue to encourage others to pray, desire, and expect their own miraculous answers from Him.

I challenge you to do that right now.

CHAPTER 10

Do Something

I OFTEN SEE God do miraculous things as I travel and minister. But there are times while ministering when I leave a ministry venue and return home without really knowing who received healing or experienced some other miraculous outcome in a service.

Sometimes people contact me later to tell me how God moved in their lives. Sadly, however, even though I and others may know God moved in a powerful way in people's hearts and lives during a particular service, I may never find out exactly what He did for them.

But we can of course confidently leave those results to the Lord. After all, He's the one who produces them.

Sometimes the miracles God performs take place instantly, and we see them as they happen. There is no doubt about those results; they are right there before us. But at other times the evidence of miracles is not immediately apparent. For instance, there are many times when people receive miracles of healing, but the results of those miracles are only confirmed later—and sometimes in progressive healings over time.

Regardless of how or when we receive or recognize the Lord's miraculous work, though, it's time for excitement. God's blessings in our lives always merit praise and thanksgiving for what God has done! But our response should go well beyond both verbal and inwardly expressed thanks for the miraculous ways God meets our needs.

If we are truly thankful, our gratitude will turn into action.

This past year I preached in a particular series of revival services at a church, and a lady responded in one of those services to the altar call for physical healing. She told me that during an examination her doctor saw something in her colon that he did not like. She said she had an appointment to see her doctor again in just a couple of days.

She was likely facing surgery to remove tumors from her colon, and the doctor told her that it was possible that a section of her colon would need to be removed—which would then require her to have a colostomy. She was very upset and scared, as could be expected. I prayed for her and asked God to completely heal her.

I was still in town preaching the week-long revival services when she called the church's pastor from her doctor's office. She asked him to tell me that she would be in the service the next night, because the doctor said there were no tumors in her colon!

Her doctor couldn't understand it, but we certainly did. I was so excited for her, and I was glad that I was still in town to hear about the doctor confirming the results of her miraculous healing.

She was thrilled, and of course I was thrilled as well.

The very next night—the last night of the services—she came up for prayer once again, and she was baptized in the Holy Spirit. She later told me that she had been seeking the infilling of the Holy Spirit for many years. I believe that receiving a miraculous healing helped build her faith and made it easier for her to receive the baptism of the Holy Spirit.

Her faith was inspired, and in gratitude for what the Lord did in healing her, she responded by obediently pressing in—doing more, stepping forward—to receive what God still had in store for her.

But the miraculous way God worked in that lady's life did not just build *her* faith, it also inspired the faith of others in the church.

That last night of the services was the most powerful night we experienced, and true revival was birthed through the testimony of that one miracle as others gave thanks to God for His wonder-working power and then stepped forward themselves into God's blessings.

God honors faithful and thankful responses. He is so good!

More recently a lady from a women's conference I spoke at contacted me through Facebook. At the conference she showed me a list of prayer requests she had written down and tucked into her pocket. That handwritten list looked like a roster of impossibilities. She had some pretty big requests, and we both knew it would certainly take a miracle for much of the list to be resolved.

I prayed for her there at the conference and called out each request to God as we agreed with one another. As we parted ways I assumed I would never hear about that encounter again, so I was surprised to receive a Facebook message from her. When I opened the message and began to read, I could sense her excitement in the words she wrote.

She informed me that she had just found the prayer list. When she unfolded it she became extremely emotional when she realized that God had answered every single prayer. She went on in her message to tell me how each one was answered.

There is nothing more exciting than hearing praise reports about the miracles God performs. And certainly it is gratifying to have people contact me and thank me for praying for the miracle they received. But my joy and gratification yields to reason and humility when it comes to representing *the Miracle Worker*.

I of course play only a small role in bringing to people their miracles. God is the one who is the miracle worker, and I am always sure to let people know they have a responsibility to give God the glory and provide to Him the proper response due *Him*.

And to be clear, what is due Him is a thankful, tangible response on our part. I strongly believe the degree to which we are truly thankful for what God does in our lives is ultimately expressed through our actions—through what we do in response to what God does.

When I consider proper responses to God for the wonderful things He does in our lives, I think of the story of the ten lepers from chapter seventeen of the Gospel of Luke.

Now on his way to Jerusalem, Jesus traveled along the border between Samaria and Galilee. As he was going into a village, ten men who had leprosy met him. They stood at a distance and called out in a loud voice, "Jesus, Master, have pity on us!"

When he saw them, he said, "Go, show yourselves to the priests." And as they went, they were cleansed.

One of them, when he saw he was healed, came back, praising God in a loud voice. He threw himself at Jesus' feet and thanked him—and he was a Samaritan.

Jesus asked, "Were not all ten cleansed? Where are the other nine? Has no one returned to give praise to God except this foreigner?" Then he said to him, "Rise and go; your faith has made you well." (Luke 17:11-19)

This passage presents to us an example of how even during Jesus' earthly ministry people didn't always receive their miracles immediately after making their requests known. In this case the men with leprosy were told to go show themselves to the priests. And it was only as they were obediently walking down the road toward Jerusalem to show themselves to the priests that they were healed.

I'm sure they *all* were thrilled, yet only one returned to give thanks to Jesus. I can scarcely wrap my mind around that. How could the other nine be so ungrateful?

In order to fully understand Jesus' instructions to the men and grasp the full impact of lessons we can learn from this passage in Luke, we need some background information:

Jewish law prohibited anyone with leprosy from associating with the general community. They had to be isolated from the general population and often lived as outcasts with other lepers for the rest of their lives on the fringes of towns.

It was because of the law that the men were standing at a distance from Jesus. They called out in a loud voice because that's the only legal way they could present their need to Him.

Imagine having to live like that! Imagine being separated from all your friends and family in your time of sickness. And imagine being mandated by law to yell out, "Unclean! Unclean!"[34] if anyone came near you to warn them of your disease. Can you imagine the humiliation they must have felt?

Once contracting the disease and being banned from their towns, the men were doomed to not only suffer the rest of their lives—as leprosy continued to eat away at their bodies—but also lose much of their identities as functioning members of their society.

They knew there was little hope for them, but they had heard about Jesus, and they went to Him. They called out to Him in desperation, and they knew that they were pleading for nothing less than a miracle.

---

34 "Anyone with such a defiling disease must wear torn clothes, let their hair be unkempt, cover the lower part of their face and cry out, 'Unclean! Unclean!' As long as they have the disease they remain unclean. They must live alone; they must live outside the camp" (Leviticus 13:45-46).

The law demanded that a person be taken to the priest for diagnosis when their skin showed signs of a *defiling skin disease*.[35] Following the process outlined in the Levitical Law delivered by God through Moses, if the priest determined the person's skin problem was indeed the sign of a defiling skin disease, the priest was required to send the person to live *outside the camp*.[36]

If the skin disease cleared up over time (was not leprosy or some other type of progressive disease), the person was once again examined by the priest to verify the skin problem had healed.[37]

If it had indeed healed, the law provided for the person healed to present sacrifices for the priest to offer during an eight-day process of ceremonial cleansing before the person could finally live in his home with his family.[38]

That's why Jesus told the men to present themselves to the priest.

After considering all the things that were soon to be restored to them—with the promise of returning to their families and regaining their identities as normal, productive members of society—I can imagine how the men were excited and could be laser-focused on running toward the temple to show themselves to the priest once they realized they had received their miracle.

---

35 Leviticus 13:2.
36 Leviticus 13:46.
37 The law requiring what we would now consider a "public health quarantine" applied to all serious diseases of the skin, not just leprosy (which we now know and treat as Hansen's Disease). At the time, leprosy was incurable and progressive, so there was no lifting of the quarantine for anyone who had it. But the law allowed for the lifting of quarantine for other "skin defiling diseases" that healed over time.
38 Leviticus 14:1-32.

But one of them—a Samaritan—stopped, while the other nine continued down the road to Jerusalem. He stood there looking at his clear skin, and his response became different from that of the others. He was filled with gratitude, and he did something the others did not do. He turned back, went back to where Jesus was, and gave Jesus thanks for the miracle of healing he received.

Only one out of ten felt it was more important to do something to demonstrate his gratitude to his Healer than it was to get his eight-day ceremony of spiritual cleansing started. Only one out of ten was thankful enough to put demonstrating his thankfulness to God above the enjoyment of what his healing was to bring to him.

And Jesus was disappointed that he was the only one to do something to show gratitude!

As I ponder all of this, I realize that I myself have been guilty of sometimes failing to adequately demonstrate my thankfulness for what God has done for me. And perhaps if we are being honest, most all of us have been guilty of that at one point or another in our lives.

We must be careful to be people who are full of gratitude for the miracles that have taken place in our lives. It doesn't matter if people consider them to be big or small. When God answers our prayers we should be quick to give Him the praise He is due. And our true gratitude should be revealed by what we do next.

Just as real faith is demonstrated by good deeds,[39] our gratitude for God's activities in our lives should be demonstrated

---

39 James 2:14-26.

by positive actions. And to me this is in perfect agreement with the fact that we must be doers, not just listeners.[40] Clearly, God is speaking to us when He heals us or does something else miraculous in our lives or circumstances, and we should *do something tangible* in return.

"But *what* can we do?" you might ask. "And, *how* can we do it?"

I firmly believe that if we are truly grateful for what God has done for us, and if we are willing to allow God to show us what to do in response, the Holy Spirit will provide not only direction for the expression of our gratitude but also the means for us to express it.

As I have shared many times, the greatest miracle God has done for me was when He rescued me from a life of sin. He spared me from so many foolish choices and patiently drew me back to Him by the power and unction of the Holy Spirit.

I've thought over and over, "How can I ever repay such a debt?"

As the Holy Spirit continued to disciple me in God's ways, my heart welled up with thankfulness. I began to desire to do something with the wonderful new life He had given me.

One of my first responses of gratitude was to accept God's call for me to enter the ministry. I once never dreamed that could ever be a possibility. But God provided not only the calling—the what—but also the answers to my questions—the how—as I pursued the path He paved before me.

As God continued to do more through miraculously teaching and leading me down that path, I continued to feel the need to do more in return. And as I continued to seek His will for my next

40 James 1:19-27.

steps, I eventually felt God impressing upon my heart the idea of writing a book.

I have to admit that even though I *wanted* to do more, I struggled with that idea.

I argued with the Lord and gave Him a million excuses why writing a book was a bad idea for me. I didn't think I could come up with enough material to write and fill a book. And I was certain I couldn't begin to write a book without help. I didn't know how to start, and I really didn't want to even try.

But I couldn't shake the fact that I felt it was something I should do in thankful response to what God did in my life. And just as many people were moved to revival through the testimony of one woman's healing in that church I ministered in, I thought my testimony of what God did in my life could also inspire faith and gratitude in others who read *my* story.

In time I looked into publishing options and discovered the differences between self-publishing and traditional publishing. Even though many of the articles I read were extremely discouraging when it came to the numbers of people who were actually able to be published traditionally (through a traditional publishing house)—one out of a hundred—I felt that was the route God intended for me.

But I was certainly concerned about how that could happen.

To me, it would take a miracle. And like many others, I was hesitant to begin the hard work of writing if I didn't see a reasonable path toward getting my work published. But I finally decided to just do something—or more specifically, *write* something.

I began to write a few blogs, and they were published online by *Her Green Room*, an Assemblies of God ministry for women—especially for pastors' wives. The results were encouraging, but it was no book. Someone suggested writing a Bible study, and I attempted to go in that direction; but that didn't work out.

I was at least writing something. But it was not *the something* God wanted. It eventually became clear to me that He definitely wanted me to place my testimony in a book. I was supposed to share the *miracle* of my restoration and how He can still use us even after we've made big mistakes. I just didn't think I could do it.

"Who would want to read it anyway?" I told myself.

So, I began bargaining with God to get out of it. I told Him that I wanted to be traditionally published, and that I wanted a really good editor to work on the book with me and an agent to represent me. I even told the Lord I wanted the editor and the agent to approach me so I wouldn't have to look for them.

I figured I had just made some pretty *unreasonable* requests, and that was probably the end of it.

It wasn't very long after that, though, when I received a personal message from a person whose *friend request* I had recently accepted on Facebook. I had never received a message from him before.

At first he asked me about some photos on my website and how I designed them. When I *snooped around* a bit, I found that my Facebook friend—an Assemblies of God minister in Oklahoma, L. Edward Hazelbaker—was a published author with an extensive editing background.

"Is this just a coincidence?" I began to wonder.

Our discussions eventually shifted to also using e-mail, and after discussing ministry, blogs, writing, photography and publishing options over several days, it became obvious to both of us that our meeting through social media was not a coincidence. It was indeed a divine encounter.

Before long L. Edward Hazelbaker extended a contract to me to officially become my literary agent as well as my editor (a rare two-in-one package). And we began working on my first book manuscript.

I was shocked by the way God was working things out, and I was beyond thrilled and excited. But having never worked with a professional editor, I soon realized it was going to be a painful experience. (L. Edward had warned me, by the way.) Remember, I had never written anything significant, and I had a lot to learn.

And I'm still learning.

Over time I have come to understand that the sometimes-torturous experience of being edited has just been part of the process of not only what I'm doing but what God is doing in me. God was not just building a book, He was building character and patience in me as well.

Work on the book took many months, but it was finally finished. After the manuscript was completed, L. Edward informed me that it could be a long time before we actually found a publisher, but he was going to begin submitting the manuscript to publishers for their consideration right away.

I was thinking it would probably take more like an eternity to find a publisher.

L. Edward submitted my manuscript to the first publishing house as I held my breath. He told me it could take a long time for the publishing company's staff to finish their review—before we heard anything back from them—and he encouraged me to be patient.

Honestly, I thought the publisher would take one look at the manuscript and reply, "Not interested."

But only two days after submitting the manuscript, L. Edward sent an e-mail message to me. He started his message by asking me if I was sitting down. Then he continued with the news that Bridge-Logos—the publisher—liked the manuscript and was interested in extending a publishing contract to me for my book.

I literally thought I was going to have to peel myself off the floor. I could not believe that was actually happening.

But it definitely was happening! L. Edward negotiated a great contract for me with Bridge-Logos, and my first book, *Beauty from Ashes: My Story of Grace* was officially released on February 1, 2018. To me that was just another miracle in my life, and that is why I share it with you in this book.

I always feel the need to do something tangible to demonstrate to God that I'm thankful for what He has done in my life—for saving my life and blessing me in so many wonderful ways. And I believe you will want to do something too. As you experience the miraculous power of God in your own life, I encourage you to not simply accept it and go your way down the road as you enjoy the results.

Turn back! Go back to Jesus—and do something!

Give Jesus thanks. Praise Him for what He's done. But don't stop there. Do more. And if you don't know what you can do for God, ask Him what He needs you to do. You asked Him for your miracle. Now ask Him what you can do to benefit the Kingdom in return.

We won't be saved by our good works. We are saved only by faith.[41] But believers always need to let their good works be seen to testify to their faith.[42] True gratitude creates an atmosphere God can work in to reveal to us and others even more of His miraculous power. And our actions that bring God glory for His deeds will always be honored by the Holy Spirit.

Others need to know that what God has done for us He can also do for them. People need hope. They need the good news we have to share. People need to hear firsthand that God is still the worker of miracles—that He still saves, heals, and does the *impossible.*

People need the Lord. That's the bottom line. And anything we can do to bring people to Christ—we need to do it. So if you are still wondering what you can do to put your gratitude into action for God, and you just don't have a clue what that is, I encourage you to just *do something* for Jesus.

Do something to prove your gratitude to God for reaching out to you and meeting your needs. Do something to testify of His goodness. Do something that God can use to draw others to Him.

---

41 "For it is by grace you have been saved, through faith—and this is not from yourselves, it is the gift of God—not by works, so that no one can boast" (Ephesians 2:8-9).

42 "In the same way, let your light shine before others, that they may see your good deeds and glorify your Father in heaven" (Matthew 5:16).

Just start there, anywhere, and you will eventually receive more direction for your future. Do something, and what you do might just turn out to lead to not only another great miracle in your life but also in the lives of others.

CHAPTER 11

Praise, Praise, Praise

THE PSALMIST WAS struggling, and in the pain of his struggle he wrote these words:

My God, my God, why have You forsaken me? Far from my deliverance are the words of my groaning. O my God, I cry by day, but You do not answer; And by night, but I have no rest.
(Psalm 22:1-2 NASB)

In his frustration he felt like God was nowhere to be found. But in the very next verse—with the next breath—the Psalmist worshiped God in this statement of faith and confidence:

Yet You are holy, O You who are enthroned upon the praises of Israel. (Psalm 22:3 NASB)

The teachings of the Bible reveal to us that God is indeed never far from the sufferer even in his or her darkest times, and if we will lift ourselves in our times of stress and trouble to give praise to God, we will find His presence.

Verse three is saying that God is enthroned *upon* the praises of His people. The King James Version of the Bible states that God *"inhabitest the praises of Israel,"* which means He lives *in* or dwells *in* the praises of His people. And it's because of that translation of Scripture (the wording of the KJV) that we often talk about God *inhabiting* our praise.

Regardless, though, whether we talk of God dwelling *in* our praise or being enthroned *upon* our praise, I believe wholeheartedly that praise fosters an atmosphere in which God will do the miraculous. God is not far from you even when it seems so—and neither are the miracles God wants to perform.

God desires our praise, and when we pour out our praise to Him and worship Him with all our hearts, I believe He moves on our behalf. And when He moves, He brings deliverance to us.

> *Do not forget the covenant I have made with you, and do not worship other gods. Rather, worship the Lord your God; it is he who will deliver you from the hand of all your enemies.*
>
> (2 Kings 17:38-39)

Throughout the Bible we read of many instances when God moved and delivered people from their enemies when His people began to worship Him. We read in Second Chronicles chapter twenty that Jehoshaphat appointed worshippers to go out ahead of the armies of Judah and Jerusalem as they marched out to face their enemies of Moab and Ammon. They sang songs of praise as they marched toward their enemies.[43]

---

43 2 Chronicles 20:21.

And as they continued to sing and praise the Lord, the armies of their enemies actually destroyed one another.[44]

When the men of Judah and Jerusalem arrived at where their enemy had assembled there was no longer an enemy to fight, so they simply collected their plunder. There was so much equipment, clothing, and other articles of value left on the ground by the defeated army that it took three whole days to collect it all.[45]

They received a miracle of victory, and the only meaningful part any of them played in bringing about that miracle was to worship and praise God.

Then we read in the book of Acts that when Paul and Silas were thrown into jail they began to pray and sing hymns and worship songs to God.[46] As they did, a strong earthquake shook the foundations of the prison.

All the doors flew open, and all the prisoners' chains fell off. As a result of that miracle, the jailer and his entire family came to know Jesus.[47] It was a miracle, and the miracle was birthed out of praise and worship to God.

Praise is indeed a powerful thing when it comes from a sincere heart that glorifies God and seeks to please the Lord.

I spoke in a large church one Sunday morning, and God moved in a tremendous way. Many people were baptized in the

---

44 2 Chronicles 20:23.
45 2 Chronicles 20:24-25.
46 "About midnight Paul and Silas were praying and singing hymns to God, and the other prisoners were listening to them" (Acts 16:25).
47 Acts 16:33-34.

Holy Spirit with the evidence of speaking in tongues. At the end of the service there was a long line of people waiting to talk to me. They were gracious and wanted to share what God had done for them in the altar service.

I noticed a lady toward the end of the line with tears streaming down her face and with her hands still lifted in praise to God. When she finally got to me she told me that she had enjoyed the service, and she was thrilled because she had been baptized in the Holy Spirit.

"But I am really disappointed" she said, "because I won't be here tonight for the healing service. I have to work, but I am so thankful to God for what He did this morning I can hardly contain my praise!" (I was planning to speak on healing that Sunday night and briefly mentioned it during that Sunday morning service.)

Almost immediately after she said those words the strangest expression came across her face. She grabbed her hip and said, "I don't know what is happening, but my hip and my leg are on fire!"

I asked her if she had been having trouble with her hip and leg. She told me she had been involved in a car accident years earlier, and she had been suffering from hip and leg pain ever since.

She said, "Ms. Donna, that is why I was really hoping to come to the healing service tonight."

I told her, "You don't have to attend a healing service to be healed. God is our Healer no matter where we are and no matter what time it is."

As tears rolled down her face, the Holy Spirit revealed to me that she was indeed receiving her healing right then and there.

She didn't come to me asking for healing, and I didn't pray for her, but she was glorifying God for what He had already done in her life. I believe that God was honored by her praise and healed her right there in the midst of it!

I then remembered a similar situation that I myself experienced several years earlier when I was attending a women's conference. I really didn't want to attend the conference, because I had been having a lot of knee pain. I avoided stairs at all cost because it was so painful to attempt to climb or descend them. I took the elevator the entire first day of the conference.

During the service on the second day of the conference the worship team began to sing a powerful song. I'm not certain of the lyrics now, but somewhere in the song it talked about jumping in praise to the Lord.

Everyone around me was bouncing like Mexican jumping beans. At first I was cringing at the thought of hopping up and down because I knew how bad it would hurt my knee. But I heard the Holy Spirit whisper in my ear, "Don't hold back your praise!"

After we sang the chorus a couple of times I decided I was going to *praise past the pain.* As I began to pour out my praise to Jesus, I found myself leaping for joy along with everyone else. And then to my amazement, I realized my knee was no longer hurting.

After the service I was able to take the stairs with no problem whatsoever. I could have probably run up and down the stairs if I had wanted to—all pain was gone! I believe God healed my knee in response to my praise. I have not had any more trouble with my knee since that day—over eight years ago.

I didn't really *feel* like praising God at that particular moment, and I certainly didn't feel like jumping up and down. But I believe God inhabited my praise and brought healing to my body.

Many good things come to us in response to our proper attitudes toward God and the praises we offer to Him. But there are times in the seasons of life when we just don't feel like praising God. We may have been hurt. We may have been rejected or experienced loss. But in any event we simply don't feel praises welling up within us in the midst of our pain.

Sometimes our experiences don't foster feelings of praise. However, even in those times—perhaps especially in those times—offering praise and thanksgiving to God is exactly what we *should* do.

I once received an inquiry about appearing on a well-known Christian television show in Canada. And there was a possibility that I would also have the opportunity to appear on another popular show that was going to be filmed in Canada while I was there. I just knew that God had planned those two opportunities and dropped them in my lap.

There wasn't a doubt in my mind!

I simply had to fill out an application to appear on the first TV program, provide three references, and supposedly it would be done. I was so excited that I immediately filled out the application and returned it. Unfortunately, a couple of weeks later I received a reply that informed me that they were not interested in an interview with me on the show at that time.

The exact words were:

The request of our CEO is to move away from featuring authors and ministries and instead specifically research for and schedule guests to share their own personal salvation testimony.

I was crushed. But if that wasn't discouraging enough, I noticed that one of my author-friends had just made an announcement that she *would* be appearing on the show!

Despite the explanation provided by the network coordinator, which said they were moving away from interviewing authors, they still chose her to appear. Because of that, I felt they were just singling me out for rejection for some other reason that they weren't saying.

Having to deal with the feeling they were being unfair in their rejection message was bad enough. But what made the experience even worse for me was the fact that since I would not be traveling to Canada for the first TV appearance, it closed the door for me to appear on the second show too.

I was so sure that opportunity had all been set up by God, so I couldn't understand why it all fell through.

At that moment I could have chosen to feel offended by God for what He had allowed to happen. I could have chosen to be upset with Him because I was rejected while another author was accepted. I could have hung my head and felt sorry for myself and chosen to wallow in self-pity.

But instead, I decided to praise Jesus!

I congratulated my author-friend on her opportunity to appear on the show—I truly was happy for her—and I praised my

Savior. And if I received nothing else at the time through my response, I received from God the miracle of peace in a time of confusion.

I have learned through several lessons that when we don't get the things we want it's not always due to rejection, but instead *redirection*. God knows best.

When I began to think about all the ways God has already blessed me it was easier to praise Him throughout my time of disappointment. Focusing on our blessings instead of our troubles, and continuing to acknowledge and appreciate the worthiness of the *God of all Blessings* in any challenging time, are keys to living a life that radiates praise.[48]

We can choose to be people who focus on the negative and build correspondingly negative attitudes, or we can be people who choose to praise God in spite of disappointments as we rise above them.

We can choose to dwell on painful moments of rejection in the present and be overcome by them, or we can continue to celebrate what the Lord has already done in our lives and live in anticipation for the miracles that are still to come.

We read in Proverbs that *"a cheerful heart is good medicine, but a crushed spirit dries up the bones"* (Proverbs 17:22).

You and I need to do everything we can to maintain and cultivate a cheerful heart and not allow a crushed spirit to dry us up!

---

48 "Praise be to the God and Father of our Lord Jesus Christ, who has blessed us in the heavenly realms with every spiritual blessing in Christ" (Ephesians 1:3).

When we look beyond our present challenges and maintain focus on the goodness of God and a vibrant relationship with our Savior, we will feel free and confident in worshiping Him. Our praise and worship will help us hear more clearly the voice of the Holy Spirit as He leads us in the direction we should go.

And I strongly believe that when praise is joined with repentance, it has the power to break chains of bondage in our lives and set us free from the strongholds of the enemy.

I and the ladies to whom I minister in jail recently experienced a very powerful jail service. Going into the service, I really had no idea what direction the Holy Spirit would lead me to take in ministry that day. As we began the praise and worship part of the service, I began to ask God for direction and to show me exactly what He wanted me to share with the ladies.

As we were singing the song *Chain Breaker*,[49] the Holy Spirit spoke to me and told me there was someone in the service who was extremely bound by the chains of sexual abuse she had experienced early in her life. The Lord made me aware that the individual was having a particularly painful day trying to deal with those memories.

I began to pray and ask the Lord to show me how to proceed. We took our seats as the song ended, and I began to speak what the Holy Spirit gave me to say to them. I told them that some of them were bound by the abuses they experienced in their past.

---

49 *Chain Breaker*, a song written by Jonathan Lindley Smith, Mia Fieldes, and Zach Williams, performed by Zach Williams on the album Chain Breakers, Essential Music Publishing, 2016.

As I continued talking, one lady began crying uncontrollably and fell forward onto the table before her. Several others followed suit. I then gave an altar call for them to repent and allow God to break the chains of guilt, shame, and the painful memories of their past.

Almost everyone responded, and I prayed with them. Later we talked about how praise helps us overcome the enemy. I explained that the enemy and his followers despise it when we lift up our praise to God, and we need to defeat his efforts and overcome the negative influences of our past through our praise and worship.

We sang one last song, and as those broken ladies lifted their voices and their hands in praise, I could almost hear the chains falling all around the room. Some wept as they sang, while others just sang softly and basked in the presence of the Holy Spirit.

Deep emotional wounds were being healed, and the enemy had to flee.

I think we often fail to realize that our praise is not just something we do; it is also a weapon we can use against the enemies of our souls. Here's something the apostle Paul said about spiritual weapons:

For though we live in the world, we do not wage war as the world does. The weapons we fight with are not the weapons of the world. On the contrary, they have divine power to demolish strongholds. We demolish arguments and every pretension that sets itself up against the knowledge of God, and we take captive every thought to make it obedient to Christ.

(2 Corinthians 10:3-5)

To me, praise is one of the main weapons we can use in our warfare against influences, situations, and circumstances that discourage and demoralize us—and against Satan and others who seek to oppose us in living victorious lives.

We take captive every one of our thoughts—especially those negative and painful ones—and make them obedient to Christ. We fill our thoughts with thankfulness and praise. Strongholds are broken when we lift our praise to God, speak and pray the Word of God, and worship Him with all our might.

In our praise, chains fall to the ground broken by the power of God. Freedom is found, and lives are forever changed. I can't imagine a greater miracle than when people are set free from the power of darkness and begin to walk in the light of Christ. And that is the miraculous nature of praise!

We should never cease to give God praise. We need to face every day viewing it as a new opportunity to offer praise to our King. Jesus truly deserves all the glory and praise we can ever express—and much more.

God blesses us, but we don't worship Him to receive blessings. And even though receiving blessings is one of the benefits of serving Him, we don't simply praise Him because of what He's done for us. We praise our Lord because we know He alone is worthy of our praise.

So in spite of every difficult circumstance, in spite of everything, we praise Him!

Think of the prophet Habakkuk again. (I mentioned him in a previous chapter.) Habakkuk was distraught by what he saw happening in his nation. The nation was under judgment by God. The hammer was falling, and nothing about it seemed fair in Habakkuk's eyes.

Habakkuk made his complaint to God and listened as God made His reply. Even after hearing God's reply and accepting that God's justice is righteous and always deserved, Habakkuk was still not a happy man. He was still filled with sorrow. But he didn't allow his sorrow to hold him back from praising and worshiping God.

Habakkuk's days were troubled. But in the midst of all of it he wrote the following (I used this quote earlier, but I use it again. It's important enough to repeat. Let it sink in):

> *Though the fig tree does not bud*
> *and there are no grapes on the vines,*
> *though the olive crop fails*
> *and the fields produce no food,*
> *though there are no sheep in the pen*
> *and no cattle in the stalls,*
> *yet I will rejoice in the Lord,*
> *I will be joyful in God my Savior.* (Habakkuk 3:17-18)

Habakkuk came to the right conclusion. He determined to not let circumstances get in the way of the praise he had to offer up to God. And it made all the difference in his outlook for the future. It provided him with a spiritual freedom and confidence that he would not have been able to otherwise experience.

We are blessed with the opportunity to offer praise to Jesus. We have many things to be thankful for, but none of those things are more important than simply knowing who He is and understanding His love for us. God is not only our creator and master of the universe; He is our Savior and sustainer.

God is not limited when it comes to His love for us and the miraculous ways He demonstrates it. So let's put no limits on our praise and the way we respond to Him with our love in return. Let us be people who delight in giving Him our praise. And let's do it again and again.

We'll experience miraculous results when we do.

CHAPTER 12

Relationship with the Holy Spirit

AS I WRITE this we just celebrated Christmas, and I had a wonderful time with family and friends. My husband gave me a very unique gift this year. When opening the package I couldn't imagine what it could be.

I admit I was a bit confused when I pulled a wooden bracelet out of the box. But when I flipped it over I noticed a small mustard seed embedded into the carved wood. That bracelet is a subtle reminder that we need faith only the size of a mustard seed to move mountains.[50]

I often still need that reminder.

---

50 "Truly I tell you, if you have faith as small as a mustard seed, you can say to this mountain, 'Move from here to there,' and it will move. Nothing will be impossible for you" (Matthew 17:20b).

Faith is necessary of course. We must have faith. We read in Hebrews that without faith it is impossible to please God.[51] We must have faith in order to believe in God, and we especially need faith to believe that Jesus' sacrifice provided full payment for our sins and paved our way to eternal life with Him.

That faith leads us to repent and accept Him as our Savior. And as our faith grows after establishing a relationship with the Lord, it leads us to fully appreciate and participate in God's miraculous plan for our lives and the lives of others.

When I first began praying and asking God to heal those in need and perform miracles for them, I often wondered if there was a specific way to do it.

I didn't know if I should pray a certain type of prayer or repeat a particular phrase. I didn't know if there was a specific amount or kind of faith I needed to possess, or if the people asking me to pray for them needed to be hyped up or inspired in some way to have a vast amount of faith.

I just didn't know much at all to be honest.

I had observed so many different ministers pray for people to receive healing, and it seemed almost every one of them had a different method. When I prayed for others and didn't see them receive their healing, I began retracing every move I made and every word I said.

"Did I do something wrong?" I thought to myself. "Do I lack the faith to see the healing manifested? Do I just not have *what it*

---

51 "And without faith it is impossible to please God, because anyone who comes to him must believe that he exists and that he rewards those who earnestly seek him" (Hebrews 11:6).

takes to minister to people in this way? Surely it must have been a lack of faith on my part!"

But then I remembered that we need faith only the size of a mustard seed. I knew I had *that* much faith.

"I believe without a doubt that God created the heavens and the earth," I told myself. "And I believe with all my heart that Jesus is the Son of God, and His blood has washed me clean.

"I had enough faith to receive the baptism in the Holy Spirit evidenced by speaking in tongues, and I had faith to pray for many others to see them receive the baptism in the Holy Spirit.

"If I had that much faith," I thought, "surely *that* was more than the size of a grain of mustard seed. I should be able to move mountains! So why am I not seeing more miracles?"

Then as I began to study the lives of some of my favorite evangelists—many of whom had tremendous healing ministries—I began to notice a common thread. All of those ministers indeed had faith, but what they talked about more than anything else was their relationships with the third person of the Trinity—the Holy Spirit.

Growing up, I was aware of the concept of the Father in heaven and Jesus the Son. That all made perfect sense. It was easy to picture a father and son, but it wasn't so easy for me to understand the Holy Spirit's position.

I heard the third person of the Trinity spoken of most often as an "it." I heard many people pray to God the Father and God the Son, but God the Holy Spirit was not mentioned in the prayers I heard. And when He was mentioned in church, it was usually in the context of coming to the altar to receive *it*—the Holy Spirit.

But as I matured in my faith I came to understand that the Holy Spirit is certainly not an "it." The Holy Spirit is a "him," and *He* is the third person in the Trinity. The Holy Spirit is God, and He should be treated with the same respect we give to the Father and the Son. When the Holy Spirit comes to us, God comes to dwell *with* us and be *in* us.[52]

We experience God's presence in a new and fuller way when we are baptized in the Holy Spirit—as He empowers us for victorious living and ministry. When we are baptized in water, we are baptized by another believer as a testimony and witness to our new birth in Christ. But when we are baptized in the Holy Spirit, we are immersed not in water (truly an it) but in the Holy Spirit—God's Spirit.[53]

We are immersed in *Him*!

It should go without saying—but I'll say it anyway—God wants to have a rich and full relationship with us. And speaking of the Holy Spirit, Jesus said to His followers:

52 "If you love me, keep my commands. And I will ask the Father, and he will give you another advocate to help you and be with you forever—the Spirit of truth. The world cannot accept him, because it neither sees him nor knows him. But you know him, for he lives with you and will be in you. I will not leave you as orphans; I will come to you." (John 14:15-18).

53 "After his suffering, he presented himself to them and gave many convincing proofs that he was alive. He appeared to them over a period of forty days and spoke about the kingdom of God. On one occasion, while he was eating with them, he gave them this command: 'Do not leave Jerusalem, but wait for the gift my Father promised, which you have heard me speak about. For John baptized with water, but in a few days you will be baptized with the Holy Spirit. . . . But you will receive power when the Holy Spirit comes on you; and you will be my witnesses in Jerusalem, and in all Judea and Samaria, and to the ends of the earth'" (Acts 1:3-5, 8).

But very truly I tell you, it is for your good that I am going away. Unless I go away, the Advocate will not come to you; but if I go, I will send him to you. (John 16:7)

Jesus actually told His followers that it was better that He go away so that our Advocate—the Holy Spirit—could come to us. We should never undervalue the importance of our relationship with the Holy Spirit.

We know the Holy Spirit as our helper, our comforter and friend, and our teacher, who leads, guides, and empowers us. But do we really understand and fully accept that the Holy Spirit is God?

Jesus was born in a manger and became *God with us.* We accept that. However, Jesus ascended back into heaven after doing His work in the flesh, and He is no longer with us in the same way He was with His followers on earth.

But God wants to be with us, to remain with us. So after Jesus ascended—after He bodily left the earth—God sent us the Holy Spirit. And now the Holy Spirit himself is also *God with us.*

Jesus is now personally working in our lives through the Holy Spirit as we go about our daily activities and do His work. And knowing this challenges me to understand more about my relationship with the Holy Spirit.

For so long I thought it would be wrong or sacrilegious to talk to the Holy Spirit in prayer. I thought it was only acceptable to speak to Jesus or the Father when praying.

And it seemed natural for me to more casually speak to Jesus or the Father while I went about my daily activities—without being in a state of focused or extended prayer—but not to the Holy Spirit.

I often offered a quick petition to Jesus to help me with this or that. And I often spoke a word of praise to let God know what a good Father He is. But even while knowing the Holy Spirit was with me, I never spoke directly to Him.

But I felt like I wanted to.

Fearful of doing something wrong, one day I asked God about it. I simply asked Him to show me the truth about talking to the Holy Spirit.

My mind was immediately taken back to one of my classrooms in elementary school. I could see my teacher at the front of the classroom. I remembered her asking us if we had any questions. In that moment it hit me.

"The Holy Spirit is our teacher.[54] When we don't understand something, we ask the teacher," I considered. "How can you ask a teacher something if you don't speak to him?"

So I began talking to the Holy Spirit. Both verbally and in my thoughts, I consciously invited Him to have a relationship with me that allowed me to be taught all the things I needed to know. And when I began honoring Him by asking Him questions, I found that He was more than willing to answer them.

As our teacher, we can trust the Holy Spirit to teach us only the truth, for He is the *Spirit of truth*.[55] And of course like any

---

54 "But the Advocate, the Holy Spirit, whom the Father will send in my name, will teach you all things and will remind you of everything I have said to you" (John 14:26).

55 "But when he, the Spirit of truth, comes, he will guide you into all the truth. He will not speak on his own; he will speak only what he hears, and he will tell you what is yet to come" (John 16:13).

good teacher, He also corrects us when we are in error. He is the Spirit of truth, so He desires to lead us into *all* truth.

The Holy Spirit reveals to us the wisdom and the insight of the Father, and He opens our understanding to Scripture. He enlightens our minds to understanding and illuminates the Word of God to speak to us, train us, and correct us.

While the New International Version of the Bible uses the word *Advocate* to refer to the Holy Spirit in the seventh verse of John chapter sixteen, the translators of the King James Version used the word "Comforter." And many of us have grown up with that title for the Holy Spirit.

When we are upset or hurting we often long for the arms and affection of our closest friend. In my case, I picture my husband holding me and telling me everything is going to be okay, as he has so many times. If the Holy Spirit is our *comforter*—and He certainly is—we should expect Him to do the same for us.

As our advocate, the Holy Spirit represents our needs and supports us in every way. And that includes helping us deal with all the things we experience. He comforts us in our times of loss, sadness, and distress. He comforts in a way that is deeper than any physical comfort we can receive from others. He provides peace that transcends understanding when we can't even understand what we need.[56]

The Spirit of God knows us better than we know ourselves. He dwells in us, and He understands us from the inside out. We

---

56 Philippians 4:7.

never have a thought that He doesn't know or consider. And His great love for us compels Him to comfort us in our times of need.

The translators of the Revised Standard Version used the word "Counselor" to refer to the Holy Spirit.[57] And indeed, one of the responsibilities of an advocate is to counsel and guide someone through situations and circumstances. The Holy Spirit leads and guides us.

I remember so many vacations I have enjoyed with my family when we have taken guided tours. We have toured caves, castles, and other destinations that require a knowledgeable guide. We were taking a tour at Mammoth Caves in Kentucky one day when our tour guide suddenly turned out all the lights in the cave.

I could not believe how dark it was. I couldn't see my hand in front of my face.

I remember thinking, "If our guide left us right now we would never get out of here."

It would have been total chaos with fifty or more people groping around in pitch black darkness. I'll admit, I felt a bit relieved when he turned the lights back on.

I can't imagine going through life without the guidance of the Holy Spirit. He is like our tour guide on this journey through life. And He continually illuminates every step of the path He prepares for us.

The Holy Spirit is completely knowledgeable about all the pitfalls and snares we might face. He helps us to weather storms,

---

57 While the Revised Standard Version contains the word "Counselor" in John 16:7, the New Revised Standard Version uses the word "Advocate." The word *advocate* is now the predominant translation of the original, "paraclete," in modern translations of the Bible.

and He gives us wisdom to make the right decisions. And like the tour guides I have been acquainted with on vacations, as the Holy Spirit guides us He loves to interact with us along the way.

The Holy Spirit is not a dull or silent guide. He desires interaction with us.

But beyond the words used by Bible translators to help us understand how the Holy Spirit is our advocate—and what that means to us—the Holy Spirit goes beyond representing us, comforting us, teaching us, and guiding us. He empowers us!

This is the big one. The Holy Spirit enables us to do what most people would consider impossible. He empowers us to do even what we ourselves often think is impossible.

Looking back on my own life—just ten years ago, before God called me into ministry—the thought of speaking in front of a group of people would cause me to break out in a cold sweat and start feeling nauseous.

But as God began to show me what He was calling me to do, the Holy Spirit also began giving me boldness and empowering me for service. A boldness I had not known before came over me.

Even when I didn't know exactly what to do or how to do it, the Holy Spirit birthed within me an intense desire to step out into the unknown and pursue all that God had for me to do. And as my relationship with God's Spirit grew, so did my confidence in the Holy Spirit's miraculous nature.

I believe when the Holy Spirit empowers us to do something, He gives us a passion for that very thing—an intense desire to see it come to fruition no matter what the cost. I can speak only of my own experience, but that is what happened when God began to empower me.

If we don't desire to do something with all of our hearts, we won't usually do whatever it takes to see the thing through.

I can't tell you how many diets I have tried and failed. Each time, I really wanted to lose the weight. Unfortunately, I didn't want to lose the weight as much as I wanted that piece of pie, that piece of cake, or that trip to the Chinese buffet! If we truly have a desire or a passion for doing something, we will do whatever it takes to realize our goal.

The Holy Spirit births goals within us and then helps us to reach them. And it has been my experience that the passion or desire He implants in my heart has also come with an equal amount of boldness to accomplish it.

Since God's power is not limited, there also is no limit on the Holy Spirit's ability to empower us to fulfill God's will in our lives. So accomplishing the things that the Holy Spirit leads us to accomplish is often just a matter of us being willing and determined to persevere.

After we understand that the Holy Spirit is indeed the third *person* of the Trinity—that He is God—and after we understand the things He does for us, we can see Him as He truly is. But I want us to go farther in understanding our relationship with the Holy Spirit.

We need to understand that He is not only what we've already discussed. We need to understand that He is our *friend*.

Jesus spoke amazing and powerful words to His followers about His relationship with them from His own perspective.

My command is this: Love each other as I have loved you. Greater love has no one than this: to lay down one's life for one's friends. You are my friends if you do what I command.

I no longer call you servants, because a servant does not know his master's business. Instead, I have called you friends, for everything that I learned from my Father I have made known to you.

You did not choose me, but I chose you and appointed you so that you might go and bear fruit—fruit that will last—and so that whatever you ask in my name the Father will give you.

(John 15:12-16)

Jesus told His disciples that He viewed them as His friends.

Jesus is of course so much more than a mere friend, yet He showed His followers that's what He wants to be to them. In addition to that, though, Jesus also said He learned from the Father what He made known to His followers. And since Jesus is a reflection of the Father, that means the Father also wants to be our friend.

But beyond even that, since there is never any separation between members of the Trinity in what they do or how they think, the Holy Spirit by mere default wants to be our friend too.

We must not see the Holy Spirit as some drifting vapor that is detached and untouchable. The Holy Spirit lives within Christians. He longs to interact with us daily. And we not only have the right to talk to Him and fellowship with Him but also acknowledge and address Him as our greatest friend.

When we find a friend who proves to be trustworthy, it is a pleasure to spend time with that person. We find ourselves opening up more and more to that person and sharing details of our lives that we wouldn't share with just an acquaintance. We learn each other's characters, and a level of trust is built between us.

We know how our friends will likely respond to things we say to them. We come to understand each other's dreams and goals, and the greatest friendships develop when we have similar goals and interests. The more time we spend together, the more comfortable we become with each other.

We feel like we can truly be ourselves with our friends without them thinking we are weird or strange.

Our friends understand us, and the same applies to our relationship with the Holy Spirit. Since He is God, He of course already understands *us*. Our challenge—and what should become our joy—is to come to understand *Him*. And that is only accomplished in our complete and full relationship with Him.

Truthfully, we can be as close to the Spirit of God as we want to be. James wrote, *"Come near to God and he will come near to you"* (James 4:8a).

Closeness in our relationship with God comes by spending time in His presence. If we want to be close to the Holy Spirit, who empowers us to do the impossible, we must be willing to spend time with Him. And we spend time with Him by praying, by resting in His presence, and by reading the Word of God.

And by talking to Him.

As we spend quality time with God we begin to recognize the voice of the Holy Spirit more clearly. We begin to trust the

Holy Spirit more fully. We come to understand His character and the part He is meant to play as the third person of the Trinity. And if we continue to grow in our relationship with Him it should be inevitable that we sense when He is leading us into and empowering us for ministry.

If we will speak to the Holy Spirit, He will speak to us. And He will lead us to pray for the sick, tell us what to do, reveal to us what to say, and inspire us to believe God for the miracles He wants to work in people's lives.

In many of Kathryn Kuhlman's services the Holy Spirit simply revealed to her what God was doing. Many times she pointed to a section of the congregation and said something like, "Someone over here has received his sight." Then that person would typically stand and testify to the fact that he had been healed of blindness.

Kathryn Kuhlman had learned to trust what the Holy Spirit was doing and saying. She had a profound relationship with the Holy Spirit.

When we have a deep connection with the Holy Spirit, and we know Him and fellowship with Him on a consistent, personal level, we too can have that kind of spiritual understanding and unfailing trust in Him.

I used to minister in churches imagining what I wanted to see happen in the services. A lot of times I would leave disappointed if things didn't go as I had imagined. But things changed as my relationship with the Holy Spirit began to grow. I began to ask Him what *He* wanted to do in the services.

And He began to tell me.

As the Holy Spirit began to show me what He wanted to do, I was no longer disappointed because I could trust Him to do what He had already revealed to me.

When we truly know the Holy Spirit and rely on His power, we can lean into Him and allow Him to do what we cannot. We can try our best to pray the right words, try to build up hype and excitement, and attempt to muster up as much faith as we feel we can—to no avail—or we can simply relax and let Him do what He naturally does.

Like a close personal friend, the Holy Spirit wants to partner with us in life and ministry. He understands us. He loves us and cares for us. And He loves us to be willing to spend time with Him.

So we take our *grains of mustard seed*, plant them in our hearts, and commit them to the Holy Spirit. And as we come to know and truly fellowship with Him, our faith grows.

Our friendship with the Holy Spirit is one of the most wonderful gifts we can possess. We can know no better friend. He is our constant companion. And as our relationship with Him prospers—as we come to fully trust Him and understand His desires for us—we can confidently step into and live in the place where the *God of No Limits* resides:

In the realm of the miraculous.

Epilogue

I ONCE HEARD someone say, "All healings are miracles, but not all miracles are healings." I don't think anyone could say it better.

I have shared and talked about several types of miracles in this book, but there is no way to name all the miracles God is capable of performing. Each miracle God performs is specific to the circumstance at hand. And we could never list all of the situations or circumstances we could find ourselves in when we could need God to do a miraculous work for us or others.

God continually responds to our needs, and we can see miracles every day of our lives if we are willing to slow down and take notice.

As we begin taking notice of the miraculous things God is doing—when we acknowledge them and begin to thank Him for even the smallest miracle—we will certainly begin to see Him move in even greater ways. And when we show our appreciation for the little things, how much more do you think our heavenly Father will desire to lavish greater things upon us?

I have often been asked, "If God still performs miracles like He did in the Bible, why don't we hear more about them?"

That's a good question, and here's one simple answer I give: We've too often stopped *talking* about miracles.

God is still performing miracles. But it's not likely to be broadcast through the media. Unfortunately, in the age we live in, tragedy and disaster sells better than the message of hope. Too many people focus on the negative. And when we focus solely on the negative our heads hang too low to see any of the positive things God is doing in the world.

We need to look up and keep our eyes on Christ!

Many people—mostly unbelievers—are in denial about the miracles God has performed and continues to perform today. They refuse to believe in miracles at all, and they try to explain them away as *coincidental circumstances*.

Those who lack faith will not accept miracles because they simply do not want to believe and trust in a supernatural God. There are those in my own family who will do everything in their power to try to disprove a miraculous event rather than accept the fact that our God still heals, delivers, and works miracles.

Despite the arguments of cynics, we must continue to spread the message of hope. And that message is incomplete without acknowledging and promoting the miracle-working power of God.

For sure, there is no greater miracle than the miracle of spiritual rebirth. We need to introduce people to the miracle of salvation by sharing with them the message of redemption and new life through the blood of Jesus Christ. But we don't need to stop there. We must then share with them our stories of the other real-life miracles God is still performing today and encourage them to believe for their own.

And as for those of us who have already welcomed and embraced miracles, we too can always find encouragement by listening to others tell of the miracles God has done in *their* lives. If we take time to talk to the people God leads across our paths, we can be blessed by hearing their miraculous stories. This should be evident to you after reading this book.

In these *last* of the last days, we need to build each other up and encourage one another. We especially need to be filled with the Holy Spirit and walk in obedience to Him. We need to have faith to believe that God is *the Miracle Worker*. And when our motives are right, we can expect Him to answer our prayers and work more and more miracles in and through our lives.

Nothing is impossible for our amazing God!

The naysayers are always with us, but there are other people around us who *do* accept and acknowledge they need miracles, and many of them are desperate for someone to show them how to trust God for them. The powers of darkness they battle are evident all around us.

Who will be full of the Holy Spirit, empowered with discernment, and bold enough to stand against the demonic influences in the world? Who will call upon God to provide undeniable testimony to His authority, drive away darkness, and usher in the power of His light?

What miracles have you seen in your own life?

If everyone on earth recognized and shared one miracle from his or her life there wouldn't be a book big enough to record them all.

So has God stopped performing miracles? No! That's absurd. God lives in the realm of the miraculous. It's impossible to stop Him from being who He is!

God wants to reveal himself to us, and God certainly desires to do that by demonstrating His mighty power through healing and miracles. I believe people are desperate today to know there are solutions more powerful than all of their problems. And those solutions exist in true, legitimate demonstrations of God's power.

Let's start the process of bringing God's solutions to bear on people's needs by drawing as close to God as possible ourselves and diligently looking for opportunities to share the Gospel. Let's start asking God for more miracles and expecting Him to perform them.

Let's start looking to the *One* who is *the Miracle Worker*. And without thinking we need to help Him or perform some kind of religious calisthenics, let's simply allow Him to do what we know He wants to do. And let us praise and honor God for every miracle He provides.

Let His praise ever be on our lips!

We must embrace openings to pray for those who need miracles and seek opportune moments to bring glory to God. We must ask the Holy Spirit to lead us into places where His power can be displayed—for believers to be built up in their faith, and for unbelievers to be shown unmistakable evidence of our loving, miracle-working God.

We must also accept that God is Sovereign. He knows every detail of every need, and He knows when to act. We have a responsibility to find *His* will in matters—not the other way around. We must not get discouraged when it seems God isn't acting in the way we think He should. We must continue to trust Him and seek His wisdom.

Finally, we must persist in our unwavering belief in the miraculous, no matter what, and never give up our confidence in the Lord.

For He alone is God, and He **IS** the *God of No Limits.*

Now I invite you to pray with me.

Lord Jesus,

We thank you for all you have done for us. You gave your own sinless life to extend the gift of eternal life to those who believe. You died on the cross, and three days later you displayed your miraculous power when you rose from the dead. Your Holy Bible tells us the same power that raised you from the dead lives in us. And you tell us in your Word that we will do even greater things than you did here on earth.

Lord, help us to put our trust in *you.* Fill us to overflowing with the Holy Spirit. Help us to realize that your power is available to all those who believe. Help us to know that the same power that raised you from the dead lives inside us to enable us to do what you did and even more.

Father, help us to have the right motives. Let our lives be undeniable testimonies to your power to save, heal, deliver, and provide for your children.

Holy Spirit, give us the boldness to speak the words *you* would have us speak. Consume us with an overwhelming desire to know you more and dedicate ourselves more fully to your plans. Teach us your ways, and give us every gift we need to live lives that are devoted to God.

Let us be humble and careful to give you all the glory, God. Let everything we say and do point to *you* and your unfathomable greatness. We surrender our lives to *your* plans and purposes. Make us usable.

We love and adore you.

In your precious Holy Name we pray, Jesus.

Amen.

ALSO AVAILABLE FROM BRIDGE-LOGOS

BEAUTY FROM ASHES
Donna Sparks

In a transparent and powerful manner, the author reveals how the Lord took her from the ashes of a life devastated by failed relationships and destructive behavior to bring her into a beautiful and powerful relationship with Him. The author encourages others to allow the Lord to do the same for them.

Donna Sparks is an Assemblies of God evangelist who travels widely to speak at women's conferences and retreats. She lives in Tennessee.

www.donnasparks.com

www.facebook.com/
donnasparksministries/

https://www.facebook.com/
AuthorDonnaSparks/

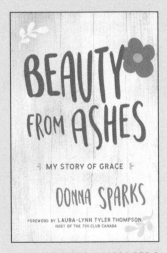

ISBN: 978-1-61036-252-8